German Recipes

German Recipes

Old World Specialties and Photography
from the Amana Colonies

Edited by
Sue Roemig Goree, Joanne Asala,
Dorothy Crum, Joan Liffring-Zug

Penfield Press

Dedicated to the generations of expert kitchen gardeners, bakers, and cooks in the seven Amana villages—Amana, East, Middle, West, High, South, and Homestead.

Connie Zuber and her mother, Mrs. Henry Moershel, at the pump in the garden back of their home. In this 1979 photograph, Connie wears a German-style dirndl typical of attire worn in the Amana family-style restaurants. Mrs. Moershel wears a dark dress and a sunbonnet typical of the Communal Era.

This collection of recipes has been made feasible by the contributions of many fine cooks and those noted with their recipes, especially Florence Rettig Schuerer, Madeline Schuerer Schulte, and Carol Schuerer Zuber. Recipes in this book are from their kitchens, from restaurants of the Amana Colonies, and from previous Amana recipe collections. A special thank you to Lanny Haldy, Director, Museum of Amana History, and to those who shared historic photographs, including Ruth Schmieder and Emily Jeck.

Front cover: *Madeline Schuerer Schulte of the Brick Haus Restaurant in Amana holds a basket of freshly baked rolls and breads.*
Back cover: *A charming scene of a rooster and hens in South Amana.*
—Color photographs by Joan Liffring-Zug.

Inside front cover: *Johanna Goerler Roemig, left, oma (grandmother) of Editor Sue Roemig Goree, is shown at a village pump with her cousin, Caroline Clemens Leichsenring, early 1900s.*
Title page: *Amana child and grapes, circa 1900.*

Cover design by Robyn Loughran.
Photographs from the collections of
Joan Liffring-Zug and the Museum of Amana History.
Associate Editors: Miriam Canter, Georgia Heald, and John Zug.

©1985, 1994 Penfield Press
ISBN: 1-57216-007-1
Library of Congress # 94-068208

Contents

*Community kitchen garden scene with women
wearing the traditional bonnets as they work with pole beans.
Cabbages for kraut are in the foreground. Early 1900s.*

Publisher's Letter

I found a warm welcome over forty years ago when I first photographed Florence Schuerer and another lady dyeing Easter eggs in the kitchen of the Colony Inn. The eggs are colored a very special way. Dye is mixed with glue from the Amana Furniture Shop. In earlier years glue was available from the shop, and the eggs came from the large flocks of chickens kept for the community kitchens, where all the people ate together until the "Great Change" of 1932.

The Amana villagers have always welcomed guests, even in the communal days when they built hotels for the visitors, particularly those coming to purchase Amana products from the woolen mill, calico print factory, and the grain mills.

Camera in hand, I kept returning to the Amanas. I have taken thousands of photographs of village scenes and have, with my editor husband John Zug, assisted in the publication of some of the colorful booklets telling the Amana story. I also collected photographs taken during the Communal Era, many of which can be found in the pages of this book.

In an emotional way, the Amanas replaced the little village of my Northern Minnesota childhood. Now I have a total of seven villages (each an hour apart by ox cart) and 1,800 people instead of 400. In 1981, I became a participant in the Amana story when my son David married an Amana woman, Carol Roemig. With the births of Jordan Hans and Forrest Paul Heusinkveld, I became an Amana *Oma* (grandmother). Carol's sister, Sue Roemig Goree, co-editor of *German Recipes,* became an aunt *(Tante)*, and in 1994 she became the mother of Katherine, the cousin of my grandchildren. Also a cousin is Madeline Schuerer Schulte, pictured on the front cover of this book. Her parents are Florence and Walter Schuerer, and so we have come full circle. I am thrilled to be a close relative and not just an admirer of the Amana Colonies and the wonderful people who live there.

—*Joan Liffring-Zug*

Above: Amana Church, 1930s.
Below: Interior of Homestead Church, 1969.

Growing Up in Amana

Sue Roemig Goree at the Amana Church, 1985.

Except for six years, I have lived all my life in the Amana Colonies. Like many others, I have strong feelings of community. It comes from two sources—the church and the extended family.

About 1,800 people live in the seven villages. Three-fourths of them are descendants of the original German religious settlers. I am one. As children, we all went to church and school together, and we shared playtimes. A feeling of community is part of growing up in the Amanas. There is a vitality, a sense of history and of faith.

The Amana religion, called the Community of True Inspiration, dates from early eighteenth-century Germany. The word *Amana* was chosen from the *Song of Solomon* in the Bible and means "to remain true." Many history-making changes have occurred over the years, but the community, as a whole, has remained true.

Communities, of course, are made up of individuals, and it is a serene experience to attend Sunday church services or evening prayer services and meditate quietly in the plain, 125-year-old sandstone meeting house. A testimony of the eighteenth and nineteenth-century inspired leaders is read. The church was founded on the belief that these leaders were the direct instruments of God, like the prophets of old. These testimonials seem timeless. The comforting thoughts or admonitions often have direct bearing on the activities of the community and on me. A sense of history envelops me as I realize that the struggles of my forefathers in the 1700s and 1800s are not unlike my struggles today.

At church, women still wear the traditional black shawl, an apron over their clothes, and a cap. Traditionally this promoted a sense of equality and humility. It's much more calming to look at backs covered with black than at bright, bold prints! Sitting on unpainted pine benches and kneeling on unpainted pine floors is so basic that it is calming. The undecorated walls are no distraction to worshipers. When Beethoven wrote the sublime *Ninth Symphony*, he turned to the fountainhead of instruments, the human voice, the musical instrument of God. I think of that, because in our church services there is no organ or instrumental accompaniment. The four-part hymns are led by a song leader.

Many of the people seated around me in church are my relatives. Traditionally, extended families lived in the same house. Some still do. When I grew up my *Oma* and *Opa* lived in the same house as my great-grandmother. If one didn't play with me or let me help, the other would. My other *Oma* lived across the street. Aunts and uncles and great-aunts and great-uncles lived within a few blocks. I really knew where I came from!

Extended families are fun and are also a great help. We always count on each other for help with showers, weddings, child care, and funerals.

One of my fondest memories is of being led to the garden in the summer by my *Oma*, who peeled a fresh kohlrabi on the spot, or offered me a handful of new peapods. *Oma* told me these were treats, and I believed her. I still love the garden treats.

While walking through the commerce-oriented streets of the Amanas, it is nice to know it remains a bustling community of families carrying on a faith.

—*Sue Roemig Goree*

Religion

The Community of True Inspiration

Church clothing,
Museum of Amana History.

In 1714 in southwestern Germany a religious movement, later known as the Community of True Inspiration, was formed. During the nineteenth century this group formed a communal society by combining all their worldly possessions and resources.

Christian Metz was the *Werkzeuge,* the inspired leader who caused the people to leave their home in Germany. The people believed that their *Werkzeuge* could receive divine guidance in the same way as the inspired prophets of old. This belief led to their persecution in Germany and the Inspirationists felt compelled to leave their home and journey to the New World.

Christian Metz told his followers, "Your goal and your way shall lead you toward the west to the land still open to you and your faith. I am with you and shall lead you over the sea." In 1842 four men were sent to the United States to purchase land. They finally settled on a tract of land purchased from the Seneca Indians near Buffalo, New York. Six villages were set up (two in Canada) and they were known as Middle Ebenezer, Upper Ebenezer, Lower Ebenezer, New Ebenezer and Kenneberg. Twelve years later, because of the rapid urbanization of the Buffalo area, four men were sent westward looking for more land. This time land was located in Iowa, just twenty miles west of the new capital of Iowa City. Over a ten-year period of time the colonists sold their land and moved to "Amana," the name for their new home.

The Amana people are not Amish and never have been. The name *Amana,* which means "remain faithful," was more than just a name to the settlers. It was a philosophy and a way of life. The Amana people

11

were able to practice their religious beliefs in an undisturbed, self-contained, communal setting.

As each of the first six villages went up, the church was one of the first buildings constructed. The seventh village of Homestead was purchased for access to the railroad. The church teaches its people to live in simple dignity and humility; likewise its structures are of plain and utilitarian design.

Church elders were once chosen by the *Werkzeuge,* but since 1883, with the death of Barbara Heinemann Landmann, there has been no *Werkzeuge* and elders have been nominated by the local *Bruderrath,* the Council of Elders, and confirmed by the Board of Trustees.

Elders conduct the church services. There once were regular services eleven times a week—morning services on Wednesdays, Saturdays, and Sundays, afternoon services on Sundays, and evening prayer meetings each day. During Holy Week there were services every day, and special services were conducted on Ascension Day, Pentecost, the Second Christmas Day, New Year's Day, and Easter. Children and young parents worshiped together, and there were also services for older people and the in-betweens, people in their 30s and 40s. Attendance by children at the evening prayer meeting was at the discretion of the parents.

Communion took place every other year. A special communion bread was baked by the village baker the day before the service. The Colonies' best wine, aged in casks for five years, was used for the *Liebesmahl* service. The children's communion was held at one of the community's kitchens, and coffee cake and hot chocolate were served instead of the bread and wine.

In 1932 the people voted for a separation of church and state, the "Great Change" from a communal society to a free enterprise system. The Amana Society was formed to operate the 26,000 acres of land and the industries. The Amana Church Society was established as a separate entity, and families began owning their own homes and making for themselves decisions which formerly were made by the elders.

The Church continues to retain a position of prominence in Amana heritage. It is the soul of the community. Its humility and dignity is still seen in the unpretentious building, the simplicity of its services, and the plainness of its cemeteries. The church has remained untouched for the most part, and except for the establishment of a Sunday School in 1931, the heritage of the past remains available for today's Amana citizens.

Photograph by Joan Liffring-Zug, 1965

Elderly member of the Community of True Inspiration
at home reading her Bible.

Never Alone
By Henry Schiff

When death came the dying were never alone. When that awesome final moment came you met it with decency and dignity. You had a doctor by your side to mark your passing. Your family gathered: immediate family in the same room; aunts, uncles, cousins, in an adjoining room. Your very closest kin would close your eyes. A hymn would be read, and prayers said. Loving hands would prepare you for burial. You would lie in state, in the room where you died, in a casket custom-built for you at the village cabinetmaker's. There would be a constant stream of people—your entire home village, as well as the other villages—to view the remains and extend their sympathy. Two of your very closest friends would "hold a wake" on your two final nights on earth. On the day of the funeral, the family would be honored luncheon guests at the kitchen that had served your needs. The *Verwandte*—the relatives— gathered at the family home an hour before the services. Then they wended their way to church in the traditional manner: first the closest male kin, then the female family/relatives. At the church entrance the entire congregation would wait; no one would enter until the *Verwandte* were seated. The service: funeral hymns, scripture, prayer, eulogy. Back home a final farewell before the casket was closed by the village cabinetmaker. The hearse—the *Leichenwagen*—a somber, black-painted, springwagon. The horses: black, groomed to a satiny sheen, always driven by the village *Gäulsboß,* the local farm manager. The pallbearers: friends designated by the family. The casket covered with a white linen sheet. The procession: first, the pallbearers and the church elders, then, in strict sequence, the male next of kin, relatives, friends, etc. In identical sequence, the female segment. Bringing up the rear, in the same sequence, the *Schulkinder,* school children with their teachers. Summer, winter, all on foot. The graveside ceremony: a hymn, the coffin lowered, a few token shovels of earth, a final prayer, and the procession dispersed—some to linger amongst the memory-evoking white markers, some to ponder life's finality on their homeward trek. The next morning the *Sterbezimmer,* the Death Room, underwent a complete and thorough ritual housecleaning to banish all taint of death.

East Cemetery, 1960s.

In each of the seven villages is a cemetery where rows of small white markers stand out in a pattern of rhythmic beauty against the dark green of the grass and the peaceful pine groves.

Each gravesite is identical in size, as is each stone marker. The dead are buried in rows in the order of death; only a few times have a wife and husband been buried side by side. In 1993 an elderly woman and her daughter were buried next to each other in the quiet Middle Cemetery. There is a special area for the burial of children.

The Amana Church teaches its members that they are brothers and sisters all, as God's children. And in death the faithful come together in final equality.

Farming the Rich Valley Land

Something strikingly different is noticed as the visitor enters the Amana Colonies. No longer are there homes or commercial buildings along the highway, but the land stretches out as far as the eye can see, broken only by highways, waterways, and fence lines, and dotted with cattle.

As it was in the beginning, all homes and barns are in the seven villages. Farming was, and is, the Colonies' largest industry. The villages were spaced several miles apart for convenience in tending the land in the days of the ox cart. Today's equipment is ultramodern; if the Colonies were being founded today, one or two villages would be enough.

The rich soil produces corn, soybeans, sorghum, oats, and alfalfa. About ten-thousand hogs and six-thousand beef cattle go to market each year.

Timber covers about half the Society's 26,000 acres. Deer, turkey, pheasants and other wildlife enjoy the Amana lands.

Colony people at lunch, circa 1900.

Henry Schmieder, great-great grandfather of Sue Roemig Goree, editor, once raised a new kind of carnation. Oldest member of the Community of True Inspiration in the 1930s, Henry Schmieder tried many new flowers.

In the early years, the Amana Church elders banned flower gardens as too worldly. As the religious rules were relaxed, Amana people planted flowers around their homes. Today, the villages are noted for their beautiful flower beds.

German Cooking in the Amanas
By Sue Roemig Goree

Even though Amana people have been thoroughly Americanized over the past 125 years, the influence of Germany is evident in Amana-style cooking. Like other European immigrants, the first Amana settlers brought their own cuisine to America and adapted it to what they could grow and what was available in their New World homes.

The German entrées such as *Sauerbraten, Wiener Schnitzel* and *Bratwurst* are perhaps more typically found in Germany's restaurants than in Amana's homes. The German influence on Amana-style cooking is more noticeable in vegetables and soups.

Rotkraut—cooked sweet and sour cabbage—is common at Amana dinner tables, and at restaurants here and in Germany. Amana-style spinach, chopped and cooked with broth, is very German. Many children dislike spinach, but Amana children often ask for it because of the flavorful way it is prepared.

Salsify or oyster plant, *Schwarzwurzel* in German, is a root vegetable still grown in Amana gardens. It is creamed and served hot. Salsify is as long as a carrot, but thinner and dark in color until it is scraped or peeled like a carrot, exposing the white. "We used to put it in buttermilk before cooking to keep the white color," said Edna Zimpleman of Amana. "We cooked it just like we cooked turnips."

Two German vegetable dishes were probably devised by thrifty cooks in some of the community kitchens. When lettuce or radishes, grown in the community gardens, were ready to bolt (go to seed), some were left for seed but the rest were harvested so that nothing was wasted. With more lettuce than was immediately needed, some cooked *Salatgemüse*. Lettuce was braised, cooked with broth and crumbs, and served hot as a vegetable dish rather than as a salad. In other kitchens, *Krautgemüse* was prepared, using cabbage.

So that none of the radishes would be wasted, *Rettichsalat* (radish salad) was prepared. Sliced radishes were served with a sour cream dressing. Some *Omas* still prepare these dishes.

German and European-style soups, hearty and meat-based, are common in Amana homes, and are often served with dumplings.

Some Amana ancestors came from Alsace-Lorraine, a province on the border of Germany and France. The Alsatians contributed a French influence to this German cooking, mainly in the form of sauces. Amana people serve a cinnamon sauce over bread dumplings, an onion sauce over potato dumplings, and cream sauces over vegetables. Bread and cracker crumb toppings are served over many dishes.

Community kitchen and workers, circa 1900. The only remaining kitchen, in Middle Amana, is preserved by the Amana Heritage Society and is open from May to October.

Daily Work

Not all women worked in the kitchens. Some were garden workers while others staffed the *kinderschule* (day care center), supervised after-school activities, did the laundry, knitted, sewed, or worked in the woolen mills.

The occupations for men were more diverse. A man could work as a barber, basket-maker, butcher, cabinetmaker, carpenter, cooper, calico factory worker, harness-maker, lumberyard worker, locksmith, mason, miller, shoemaker, storekeeper, tailor, tanner, wagon-maker, watch-maker, medical doctor or dentist, pharmacist, teacher, postmaster, etc. The colonies were self-sufficient and even the children were expected to do their share.

Community Kitchens and Gardens

Before the 1932 Great Change from a communal life style to a free-enterprise system, the Amana people ate together in the community kitchens. There were several kitchens in each village. Each served forty to fifty people five times daily—breakfast, morning coffee break, lunch, afternoon coffee break, and supper. A rotating menu was used: certain dishes or combinations were always prepared on certain days.

Women operated these kitchens. The "kitchen boss," held a position of considerable responsibility. She managed kitchen helpers, planned meals according to the amount of food harvested from the kitchen's large garden, cooked, baked, and trained new staff. A sense of urgency surrounded the kitchen work. Large quantities of food were needed and the people expected their meals to be served on time.

After completing the eighth grade at age fourteen, girls immediately went to work in the communal kitchens. New mothers were allowed a two-year leave of absence from kitchen work in order to stay home with their babies.

Fifteen minutes were allowed for each of the three main meals, while the mid-morning and mid-afternoon coffee breaks (including a snack) often lasted thirty minutes. Most people ate in silence. Men ate at separate tables from the women and children. Meals were carried home in baskets for new mothers or invalids.

Each community kitchen had its own hen yard providing eggs and stewing-hens. Beef and pork were delivered several times a week by the village butcher. Each Amana village was nearly self-sufficient.

The community kitchens were surrounded by the community gardens, also staffed by women. Besides fresh summer produce, much was grown for winter use. The kitchen boss managed the canning, pickling and drying of fruits and vegetables. Nothing was wasted. In the spring, onions and lettuce were planted first, followed by tomatoes, cabbage, squash, corn, beans, beets, peas, cucumbers, radishes, potatoes, and other vegetables.

When the community kitchens closed in 1932, nearly eighty years of community-shared meals came to an end. Cooks adapted recipes and learned to cook for single families. Kitchen appliances were installed in family dwellings.

Today's gardeners continue to plant some of the more unusual vegetables and fruits used in the Communal Era. Amana gardeners grow a variety of flat green beans and a tender leaf lettuce called *Eiersalat*. Salsify or "oyster plant," a root vegetable, is grown, as is *Knollecelerie*, a type of celery grown for the root and used in soups. Kohlrabi from the gardens is eaten cooked or raw, and leeks are grown for use in soups. Horseradish is raised and the roots are dug in the fall.

Two unusual fruits still grown are ground cherries and currants. Both grow on low bushes. Ground cherries are used for pies and jellies. Currants are tasty mixed with raspberries and cherries.

Even in tree-planting, Amana villagers were practical. Fruit trees were favored. They provided shade, the spring blossoms were enjoyed, and the fruit could be eaten. Cherry and apple trees were the most common.

Photo by Joan Liffring-Zug, 1970

Sorting spinach in one of the wooden trays used during the Communal Era.

Guide to Amana German Words

auf Wiedersehen	good-bye, until we meet again
bitte	please
danke schön	thank you
gemütlichkeit	hospitality
Oma	grandmother
Onkel	uncle
Opa	grandfather
Tante	aunt
willkommen	welcome

Kitchen workers sorting onion sets, circa 1900.

Table Graces

From the book Communistic Societies of America *by Charles Nordhoff.*

This table grace is commonly said at meals by Amana families. It is prayed in German as often as in English. One person says the prayer and a blessing is said in unison at the end.

Komm Herr Jesu,   Come Lord Jesus,
sei unsere Gast,   Be our guest
und segne was du uns bescheret hast. and let this food to us be blest.
(In unison) Amen. Gott segne uns. (In unison) Amen. God bless us.

My *Opa* (grandfather), Paul Oehl, always pointed out, in his humorous way, that if we omitted saying "God bless us" at the end, the prayer didn't count. So if you decide to use this prayer in your home, be sure not to forget that important line.

An after-dinner table grace is less common, but the one recited in many Amana homes is:

Herr Jesu, dir sei lob und drank, für die genossene Speis und Trank.

Translation: Lord Jesus, we praise and thank Thee for the nourishing food and drink.

—*Sue Roemig Goree*

Amana's Old World Christmas

Jordan Hans Heusinkveld shown in the rocking horse once ridden by his Opa. In refurbishing this antique, the rocking horse's worn tails were replaced with genuine cow tails from the Homestead Meat Market. Traditionally, horsehair tails were used.

At the Amana Colonies in Eastern Iowa, memory figures significantly in the observance of Christmas as the Amana people recall the Old-World flavor of the holidays much in the manner of their German ancestors.

Down from the attic or out of the cupboard at Christmastime come treasures saved for many years, such as handmade decorations and tabletop-sized trees with quaint, doll-sized ornaments woven of yarn. At holiday parties, voices of young and old blend in singing familiar traditional carols in both English and German. In nearly every kitchen there is a delightful aroma of things baking—*Springerle, Weihnachts Stollen* (Christmas yeast cake), marzipan and other treats, many of which find their way into decorated baskets intended as special gifts for friends and relatives.

Out of regard for their heritage and from habit of living somewhat apart from the mainstream of American culture, the Amana people have preserved some of the essential elements of Christmas as celebrated in their European homeland long before the establishment of the Iowa communities.

Perhaps the most singular reminder of the holiday's German origins is the appearance of the *Weihnachts pyramide,* or Christmas pyramid. This elaborate decoration takes the place of, or is used in addition to, the Christmas tree.

Fashioned of wood and anywhere from one foot to several feet square at the base, the handmade structure is actually a series of three or more tiers that become proportionately smaller the higher they go. On most models, there is a free-moving center post that runs from the base

Harvey Jeck of High Amana builds a pyramid in his workshop while his son Robbie watches. 1970s.

corner posts. Attached to the center post at the level of each tier are disc-shaped shelves and, at the top, a multi-bladed fan.

At Christmastime, the pyramid usually adorns a tabletop and is festooned with ornaments, Nativity figures, candles (placed in special holders attached to the framework) and, in some cases, greenery. When the candles are lit, the heat from them turns the fan blade and thus the center post and discs. The figures turning on the shelves, the glittering ornaments and the soft candlelight create a kind of enchanting Christmas fairyland.

Many of the Amana pyramids are precious family treasures that have been handed down from generation to generation. Still others are new—the handiwork of present-day Amana craftsmen who keep alive the customs of their forefathers. The older examples of this unusual Christmas architecture are usually found in the homes of people with ancestors from Saxony in Germany, for this tradition, and others, came to this country from Saxony—from the towns and villages nestled in the foothills of the Erzgebirge range, the Iron Mountains that now form the border between Germany and the Czech Republic.

Speaking as if from the past, Amana resident Henry Schiff relives part of the old country holiday celebration:

"It is the beginning of the Advent season, and we trudge through the blue December dusk to go *hutzen,* or visiting, at the traditional pre-Christmas gatherings at a neighbor's *Hutzenstub,* or family room.

"Here are the women and girls in one corner of the room with *Kloppelholz* and *Kloppelkissen,* lacemaking bobbin and lacemaking cushion, weaving the intricate gossamer lace of Saxony.

"And, at the table are the men and boys with carving knife and paintbrush, shaping, molding and renovating the sprites, pixies, shepherds, flocks...the wise men, the angels, the manger, and the image of the Christ Child—all these figures to be used in the traditional communal expression of the Christmas spirit, the *Weihnachtsberg.*"

Elizabeth Eichacker Lipman and John Eichacker with Christmas presents and doll-size model of the community kitchen. Early 1900s.

The *Weihnachtsberg* (literally, Christmas mountain) was a large Nativity scene assembled out-of-doors from figures hand-carved by townspeople. It is still featured today in some parts of Germany. Each year at the *Hutzen* evening, the men and boys of the village would repair figures from previous years and make new ones to adorn either the Christmas mountain or the Christmas pyramid. While working, they often joined in the customary *Hutzensingen,* or carol singing, in the original Erzgebirge dialect.

Over the years, the Christmas mountain assumed secular characteristics, and it was not then unusual for someone to be carving a Cinderella, a Sleeping Beauty, or another storybook favorite of German children. These fanciful creations would take their place in the display alongside the familiar Biblical characters.

Unlike its larger counterpart, the Christmas pyramid remained indoors as a more personal and individual expression of the Christmas story. The people of Saxony, it is said, favored it over the Christmas tree because they were reluctant to cut down a live tree and so waste a growing gift of God.

They used native wood in building the pyramids and designed them along lines later reflected in the Amana versions. The shelves and revolving discs held Christmas gifts and the carved figures made at the *Hutzen* evening.

Settlers in Amana from Saxony naturally preferred the Christmas pyramid, while those of different backgrounds brightened their homes with the familiar Christmas tree.

Amana resident Carl Oehl recalls an unusual tree that was part of his childhood Christmas:

"There was that special tree, made with pine branches from the nearby pine forest. On Christmas Eve, the branches were placed in holes drilled in a straight pole set in a heavy base.

"The small clip-on candleholders were attached to the branches along with the old-fashioned tree ornaments handed down from generation to generation. A Nativity display, its figures spattered with wax drippings from other years, was enclosed within an ornamental fence at the base of the tree.

"Finally candles were placed in the holders and lit as the family gathered around the tree to sing carols. The warm glow of the candles cast a dancing reflection on the wall. The scent of fresh pine and the joyful music made such an impression on us that we nearly forgot to open our gifts."

Likewise, Henry Schiff also remembers the childhood excitement upon first seeing the Christmas tree and its gifts:

"The *Rundbrenner*, or round wick kerosene lamp, had been extinguished. The only light came from the candles on the tree which rested on a table covered with white linen. The Christmas angel atop the tree touched the ceiling and the ornaments were freckled with candle wax.

"Perhaps two dozen candles decorated the branches, but rapt eyes seemed to reflect hundreds.

"Underneath was the manger, the Christ Child, Mary and Joseph. Spread over the table in a neat and orderly fashion were the gifts—never wrapped but open for immediate inspection.

"There was always a book—*Hansel and Gretel* for the very young and *Robinson Crusoe* for the older children.

"There might be a sled or skates, dolls or farm sets, doll houses or stone building blocks, and always something useful and something to wear—gloves, scarves, boots, mufflers, or leggings.

"There were fruits—oranges, apples, and bananas—and candies such as pink and white marshmallow fish, chocolate-covered mice with pink candy eyes and string tails. And always hard candy, English walnuts and peanuts.

"After church on Christmas morning, there were visits to neighbors to see 'what others got.' Then finally, on the second day of Christmas, you were alone with your treasures."

Today, the holiday celebration at Amana still retains much of this old-fashioned charm although, most likely, the Christmas pyramid shares a corner with the Christmas tree, and on its revolving shelves, toy astronauts and trucks have replaced mittens and skates.

There is one thing for certain to be very much the same—the faces of the young, wide-eyed and enchanted before the Christmas pyramid, gathering in their own memories-to-be of Christmas in Amana.

—*Joan Liffring-Zug and Charles Roberts*
The Iowan Magazine, 1975

The Amana Heritage Society

Amana girls, early 1900s.

Visitors to the Amana Colonies can learn about the community's culture and heritage at the Museum of Amana History in the village of Amana. The three nineteenth-century buildings of the Museum are set in spacious grounds amidst beautiful flowers. The Noé house building was constructed in 1864 as a communal kitchen and residence. Built in 1870, the old village schoolhouse is right next door, and the wash house/woodshed is as it was at the turn of the century, preserved so that it seems it could be used again for communal washing.

Exhibits in the Museum buildings trace the history of Amana from its religious origins in eighteenth-century Germany. The origin and structure of Amana's communal social system is explained and visitors can see what daily life was like in communal Amana. Museum exhibits also interpret the various industries and crafts of the community: woolen and calico products, baskets, tinware, and handiwork are all displayed

An award-winning audiovisual presentation is shown regularly in the auditorium of the Museum of Amana History. Using historical photographs and oral history recollections, the program strikingly presents the Amana story.

Throughout the year, the Museum is host to special programs and events that are fun and educational for both residents and visitors. Guided walking tours of Amana villages, lectures by renowned scholars,

Vine-covered, unpainted woodsheds, such as this one pictured in the 1980s, once served an essential purpose when the community kitchens used wood in the hearths, and an abundance of wood from Amana timberlands heated the homes.

special children's activities, and festivals such as *Prelude to Christmas* are all part of the Museum's annual calendar.

Genealogists, historians and local history enthusiasts can make appointments to use the extensive resources of the Museum's library and archives. Books, letters, photographs, and the manuscripts which document Amana's past are preserved and available.

The Museum of Amana History is operated by the Amana Heritage Society, a nonprofit organization founded in 1968 by residents dedicated to preserving Amana's cultural heritage for the community and its descendants. The Heritage Society has grown steadily through the years. Membership in the organization numbers over 700. The

Museum collections contain more than 8,000 artifacts. In addition to the Museum of Amana History, the Heritage Society operates the Communal Kitchen and Coopershop Museum in Middle Amana and the Communal Agriculture Museum in South Amana.

The Communal Kitchen Museum is the only intact communal-era kitchen remaining in the Amana Colonies. It is preserved as it was in 1932 when the communal system ended and the kitchen served community members for the last time. Visitors can see the large brick hearth, dry sink, and cooking utensils that were used to prepare the meals. In the dining area long tables are set—ready for mealtime. From a docent the visitor hears about the daily routine of the women who worked in the kitchens.

Across the street from the kitchen is the Coopershop where communal-era craftsmen made barrels, buckets, and tubs to serve the community's needs.

The Communal Agriculture Museum in South Amana's old horse barn displays huge posts and beams that were hewn from native lumber and joined with wooden pegs. Exhibits in the barn explain the way Amana's communal farmers cultivated the 26,000 acres of land owned by the Amana Society.

Because of their unique religious and communal history, the Amana Colonies are designated a National Historical Landmark. The Museums of the Amana Heritage Society offer the visitor to Amana a close look at life as it was in this communal society, and also provide a different perspective on American history.

—Lanny Haldy, Director
Amana Heritage Society

Visitors to the Amanas, 1920s.

*Display of handmade tin utensils from the Communal Era,
The Museum of Amana History.*

The tinsmith's shop was equipped with a variety of tools and hand-pow-
ered machines for cutting and shaping metal into whatever the community needed. The types of metal used included hot-dipped tinplate, hot-
rolled sheet steel, cold-rolled steel plate, terneplate and copper.

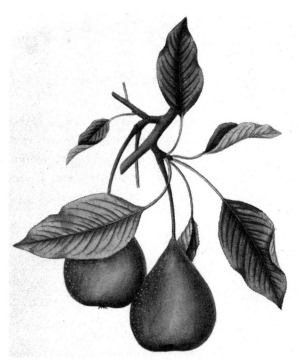

Prestele Lithographs
Museum of Amana History

Later he emigrated with the community to America. Within three years of his arrival, Joseph had acquired a reputation for exquisite botanical illustrations. His three sons, Joseph Jr., Gottlieb, and William displayed varying degrees of talent and success. Their legacy, the hundreds of lithographs and paintings, remain in books of botany, the archives of the Smithsonian Institution, and in Amana homes.

Joseph Prestele was born in Bavaria in 1796. His father was the caretaker of the estate of Count von Stauffenberg and Joseph grew up among the flower beds and orchards of Stauffenberg Castle. His love of botany was combined with his talent for lithography, and he found work illustrating catalogues of European and Asian trees and plants. He was employed by the Royal Botanical Garden as a staff artist, and earned an annual stipend from King Maximilian I. In 1835 Joseph met the Inspirationist leader, Christian Metz.

Beverages and Appetizers

The Colony Cocktail

The Colony Cocktail was discovered in the early days of winemaking when only rhubarb and Concord grape wines were made. The rhubarb is a dry wine, and the red Concord is sweeter. A third wine was created by mixing the two in equal parts to have a medium-taste wine. It was immediately called *The Colony Cocktail* and remains popular today.

White Wine Cup
Helen Kraus, from The Story of an Amana Winemaker.

5 cups rhubarb wine
3 cups orange juice
2 1/2 cups cold water
1 1/4 cups pineapple juice
1/2 cup sugar
1/4 cup grated lemon peel,
    absolutely no pith

2 tablespoons honey
6 whole cloves
1/2 teaspoon cinnamon
1/2 teaspoon nutmeg
scant 2 quarts ginger ale
crushed ice

Mix all ingredients, except ginger ale and ice. Refrigerate 3 hours. At serving time, strain, add ginger ale and pour over ice. A zippy, icy punch with sparkle. Serves twenty.

In the early years, the Colonists made their own beer. This photo shows an early 1900s outing. The Millstream Brewery in Amana, specializing in a variety of German-style beers, opened in the late 1980s.

Eier Punch
Helen Kraus

1 1/2 quarts Concord grape wine
1 quart water
1 1/8 cups sugar

juice of one lemon
nutmeg and whole cloves to taste
8 eggs, beaten

Combine all ingredients except eggs, and heat. Add beaten eggs and continue beating until frothy on top. Do not boil or mixture will curdle. Serve at once. Serves ten. A terrific egg-punch for a German-touched holiday.

Spinach Dip
Brick Haus Restaurant

1 10-oz. package frozen spinach
    cooked and drained
4 oz. cream cheese, softened
1 cup mayonnaise
1 cup sour cream

1 box leek soup mix
1 small bunch green onions,
    chopped
1 loaf French bread

In a bowl, combine all ingredients and place in a hollowed-out loaf of French bread. Cut bread from hollowed loaf into bite-sized pieces. Serve alongside to eat with spinach dip. Makes about three cups.

Holiday Cheese Ball
Linda Schuerer

2 8-oz. packages cream cheese
1/2 pound sharp Cheddar
    cheese, grated
1 tablespoon Worcestershire sauce

1 small onion, grated
1/2 teaspoon salt
1/4 teaspoon celery salt
1 cup walnuts, chopped

Soften cream cheese and Cheddar cheese to room temperature. In a bowl, combine all ingredients except nuts. Shape into one or more balls. Roll each ball in chopped walnuts. Chill until firm. Can be made up to a week ahead and refrigerated until serving time. Makes three cups.

Pork Liver Pâté
Helen Kraus

1 1/2 pounds pork liver, minced
1 1/2 cups finely ground pork
2/3 cup chopped salt pork
strong dash of nutmeg, or to taste
strong dash of oregano, or to taste
dashes of freshly ground pepper

1/4 teaspoon crushed bay leaf
3 cloves garlic, crushed
2 tablespoons brandy
1/2 cup dry rhubarb wine
uncooked bacon slices

Mix the liver, pork, and salt pork. Add the nutmeg, oregano, pepper, bay leaf, garlic, brandy, and wine; mix thoroughly. Line a terrine or any 1-quart, oven-proof casserole with bacon slices and fill with the liver mixture. Press down firmly and top with more bacon slices. Cover with aluminum foil and bake at 350° for 1 1/2 hours. Cool and refrigerate at least eight hours before serving. Serves about twelve.

Deviled Puffs
Linda Schuerer

1 cup water
1/2 cup butter

1 cup flour
4 eggs

In a saucepan, heat water and butter to a rolling boil. Over low heat, stir in flour. Continue to stir vigorously for about one minute, until mixture forms a ball. Remove from heat. Beat in all eggs until smooth and glossy. On greased cookie sheets, drop dough by slightly rounded teaspoonfuls. Bake at 400° for 25 minutes, until they are golden brown, puffed up and dry. Cool. Fill puffs with ham or tuna salad. Makes three to four dozen.

An Amana basketmaker created this willow laundry basket with removable bottom rim to replace when worn.

Soups

Potato Soup
Madeline Roemig

This is an ideal way to use chicken broth one may have on hand from cooking chicken for a salad or casserole. My family usually treated potato soup as "peasant food" and had been only slightly interested in having it served to them. I countered this by adding egg yolks and sour cream, which creates an elegant soup. To impress them further, I remind them that this might also be served cold as a very classy vichyssoise.

3 large potatoes, sliced thin
4 slices lean bacon, diced
6 leeks, sliced thin (onion may
    be substituted)
1/4 cup chopped onion

2 tablespoons flour
4 cups chicken broth
2 egg yolks, beaten
1 cup sour cream
3 tablespoons chopped parsley

Peel and slice potatoes. Sauté bacon in a deep saucepan for 5 minutes. Add leeks and onions and sauté for 5 minutes. Stir in the flour. Slowly add the chicken broth, stirring constantly. Add potatoes and simmer for 1 hour. Mix in blender or food processor until creamy. Combine egg yolks and sour cream, add to soup. Simmer for 10 minutes, stirring constantly. Garnish with fresh chopped parsley. Makes 2 quarts.

Planting potatoes, circa 1900.

Utensils, Community Kitchen Museum. Craftsmen in village tin shops made star cake pans, colanders, pails, ladles, cookie cutters and other tools.

Beef Broth

Clear beef broth is a versatile dish that can be served with liver dumplings. (Recipe for dumplings can be found on page 90.)

10 cups water
1/2 cup assorted vegetables, chopped very fine (carrots, celery, parsnip, onions, etc.)
1 bay leaf
1 to 2 teaspoons salt
1/4 teaspoon pepper
1 1/2 pounds beef chuck
1/2 pound beef bones
1 tablespoon fresh chopped parsley or chives
1/2 teaspoon nutmeg, or to taste

In a large kettle, combine water, chopped vegetables, bay leaf, salt, and pepper. Bring to a rapid boil. Add meat and bones, cover and reduce heat. Simmer 3 to 4 hours, but do not boil. Boiling will make the soup cloudy. Remove meat and bones from broth. Save the meat. The meat may be sliced and served with mustard sauce. Pour broth through a sieve into another pan. Sprinkle with parsley, chives and nutmeg and serve by itself or with liver dumplings. Makes three quarts.

Cream of Mushroom Soup

3 tablespoons butter
1 large onion, chopped fine
2 stalks of celery, chopped fine
3/4 pound mushrooms, chopped
1 teaspoon dried mixed herbs
salt and pepper to taste

2 tablespoons flour
2 1/2 cups vegetable stock
2/3 cup cream
4 mushrooms sliced lengthwise
    and fried until brown
dashes of paprika

Melt the butter in saucepan. Fry onion and celery until soft. Add finely chopped mushrooms, herbs, salt, and pepper. Cook gently until mushroom juice evaporates. Stir in flour and cook for a couple of minutes. Add vegetable stock and bring to the boil, stirring occasionally. Add cream; whisk and reheat without boiling. Garnish each bowl with mushroom slices and dashes of paprika.

Pea Soup

1/2 pound dried peas,
    soaked overnight
2 tablespoons butter
1 onion, chopped
1 carrot, diced
1 clove garlic, crushed
2 celery sticks, chopped

3 cups water
3 cups vegetable stock
1 teaspoon dried mixed herbs
salt and pepper to taste
4 tablespoons cream

Melt butter in saucepan. Add the onion and carrot and sauté gently until onion is softened. Add the garlic and celery and cook for five minutes. Drain the peas and add to the saucepan along with the water, stock, herbs, salt, and pepper. Cover and boil for ten minutes, then simmer for 2 to 3 hours, until the peas are soft. Allow to cool slightly, then liquidize with cream to a smooth paste. Add more cream or water if too thick. Reheat soup before serving.

Onion Soup

2 quarts water, salted
2 pounds small onions, peeled
2 1/2 pounds potatoes, peeled
salt and pepper to taste

3/4 pound smoked sausage, diced
1/8 pound bacon, diced and fried
4 tablespoons butter

Bring water to a boil in large stockpot. Add peeled onions and cook until tender. Boil potatoes separately and purée. Add to onions, stirring until well-mixed. Cook over low heat until thickened. Season with salt and pepper. Add sausage, bacon and butter. Serve with white bread.

Barley Soup

1/2 cup dry beans
2 cups water
8 cups beef stock
1 carrot, sliced
1 onion, chopped
1 stalk celery, sliced

1/2 cup cooked lentils
1/2 cup barley
1 8-oz. can tomato soup
1/2 cup rolled oats
1/2 cup frozen green peas
parsley, salt and pepper to taste

Soak beans overnight according to package directions. Put water and beans in a saucepan. Bring to a boil; shut off heat and let cool for one hour. Drain. Combine all ingredients in a large stockpot and simmer for two hours.

Cabbage Soup

1 1/2 pounds ground pork
    or chicken
3 to 4 cups cabbage, chopped
1/2 cup onions, chopped
1/2 cup celery, chopped

1 cup carrots, sliced
1/4 cup green peppers, chopped
1 quart tomato juice
1 cup water
1/2 teaspoon salt

Brown pork or chicken in saucepan; drain and add vegetables, tomato juice, water, and salt. Cover and simmer until vegetables are soft, about half an hour. Also may be cooked in a crock pot for 6 to 8 hours.

Salads and Salad Dressings

Oma Rettig's Dandelion
Greens with Bacon Dressing
Madeline Schuerer Schulte

Early spring dandelion greens are best as they are most tender. This recipe was used by Madeline's Oma, Louise Rettig.

4 slices bacon, diced
1/2 cup sugar
1/2 teaspoon salt
1 tablespoon cornstarch
1 egg, lightly beaten

1/4 cup cider vinegar
1 cup light cream
4 cups dandelion greens
1 hard-cooked egg, chopped

Cook bacon until crisp. Reserve drippings and bacon. Combine the sugar, salt and cornstarch and mix well. Gradually stir in the egg, vinegar and cream. Pour mixture into the bacon and drippings and cook, stirring until mixture thickens. Pour over dandelion greens and garnish with egg. Serves four.

Tart Salad
Anna Hegewald

1 11-oz. can mandarin oranges
1 14-oz. can pineapple tidbits
1 1/2 cups fruit syrup and water
1 6-oz. package orange gelatin

1 1/2 cups buttermilk
2 cups small curd cottage cheese
white miniature marshmallows

Drain the oranges and pineapple. Reserve syrup and add water to make 1 1/2 cups liquid. Heat to boiling. Add gelatin and dissolve. Stir in buttermilk and cottage cheese. Chill until thickened. Fold in drained fruits. Sprinkle with white miniature marshmallows. Serves fifteen.

Tante Anna's Cranberry Salad
Madeline Schuerer Schulte

1 pound cranberries	1 cup hot water
1 orange	1 cup celery, chopped
2 cups sugar	1 cup nuts, chopped
1 package gelatin (orange, lemon or apple)	1 8-oz. can pineapple, drained

In a food grinder, grind cranberries and orange, using everything but seeds and stems. In a bowl, mix cranberries and orange with sugar and let stand overnight. Dissolve the gelatin in the cup of hot water and let cool to lukewarm. Add to the cranberry and orange mixture. Then add celery, nuts and pineapple. Place in a 6-cup mold and refrigerate.

Fruited Chicken Salad
Madeline Schuerer Schulte

2 cups cooked chicken, diced	1 cup orange segments, halved
3/4 cup celery, diced	3/4 cup seedless grapes
1/2 cup nuts, coarsely broken	mayonnaise

Combine chicken with celery, nuts, orange segments and grapes. Mix with mayonnaise to moisten. Refrigerate and serve cold on a lettuce leaf. Serves four.

Cucumber Salad
Walt Schuerer

6 cucumbers, peeled and sliced	dash of pepper
1 onion, sliced thin	3 tablespoons vinegar
1 teaspoon salt	2/3 cup cream

Mix all ingredients and chill for 2 to 3 hours before serving. A cool treat for a hot summer's day, and a delightful addition to any picnic. Serves ten to twelve, depending on the size of the cucumbers.

Sauerkraut Salad
Walt Schuerer

1 quart sauerkraut
1 cup celery, diced
1/2 onion, chopped
1 cup sugar

1/2 cup oil
red and green peppers for taste
and color, chopped

Mix all ingredients thoroughly and serve. Serves six to eight.

Hot German Potato Salad
The Colony Village Restaurant

In a large roaster combine the following, except bread crumbs:

12 to 24 boiled potatoes,
cut into chunks
3 large onions, chopped

1 pound wieners, cut into
diagonal slices
bread crumbs, browned

Sauce:
1/2 pound margarine or butter
1 cup flour
salt to taste
2 tablespoons dry mustard

pepper to taste
8 cups cold milk
8 cups mayonnaise

To prepare sauce: Melt margarine and combine the first five ingredients. Then add milk all at once. Blend and stir over medium heat until mixture boils and thickens. Boil one minute, remove from heat. Blend in mayonnaise and mix well.

Add the sauce to potato mixture. Mix gently so as not to break up potatoes. Sprinkle with bread crumbs. Bake at 350° for one hour or until it is cooking around side of pan. This is a crowd-sized recipe.

Above: Community kitchen gardeners, early 1900s.
Below: Putting up kraut at the Homestead kitchen.

Tomato Salad with Onion and Peppers
Elsie Oehler, from the Ronneburg Recipe Album.

Color and texture make this a very appealing dish. And wait until you taste it! This is one of our most requested recipes. We use only garden-grown tomatoes when they are in season. Although "store-bought" tomatoes may be used, they will not have the flavor that homegrown tomatoes have. Yellow tomatoes may also be added. They will add even more color to the salad.

4 large tomatoes, cut in chunks	1/2 cup vinegar
1/2 green pepper, chopped	1/2 cup water
1 medium onion, sliced	salt to taste
3 tablespoons sugar	

Place tomatoes, green pepper and onion in a bowl. Sprinkle with sugar and let stand about 15 minutes. Add remaining ingredients and stir thoroughly. Refrigerate at least 4 hours before serving. This will keep several days if refrigerated. Serves four to six.

Marinated Mushrooms
Terry Roemig

1 pound fresh mushrooms	1 tablespoon Dijón mustard
1 1/2 teaspoons salt	3/4 teaspoon tarragon
3 tablespoons minced parsley	1 1/2 teaspoons sugar
3/4 teaspoon freshly ground	1/2 cup wine vinegar
black pepper	1 1/2 cups salad oil
1 clove garlic, minced	

Fill quart jar with cleaned mushrooms cut into uniform size. Combine all other ingredients in a small bowl and mix with a wire whisk or, if you dislike mincing garlic and parsley, use a food processor. Pour dressing over mushrooms; cover and refrigerate. Tip jar twice a day to make sure marinade covers all mushrooms. They are ready to eat in one or two days.

Amana-Style Sour Cream Salad
Lina Leichsenring

1 head lettuce, shredded
1 small onion, cut fine
1/2 teaspoon salt

dash of pepper
3 tablespoons vinegar
1/4 cup sour cream

Mix the onion, salt, pepper, vinegar, and sour cream; pour over shredded lettuce. Serves six to eight.

Fruited Cabbage Salad
Madeline Schuerer Schulte

2 oranges, peeled and sectioned
2 apples, chopped
2 cups shredded cabbage (green)
1 cup seedless green grapes
1/2 cup whipping cream

1 tablespoon sugar
1 tablespoon lemon juice
1/4 teaspoon salt
1/2 cup mayonnaise or
   salad dressing

Place oranges, apples, cabbage and grapes in bowl. Beat whipping cream in a chilled bowl until stiff. Fold whipping cream, sugar, lemon juice, and salt into mayonnaise. Stir into fruited cabbage mixture. Serves six.

In the Communal Era, school children maintained the orchards. These children are carrying apple baskets. Each village had a drying house for fruits.

Grated Beets

3 medium-sized beets, uncooked
1 sour apple, grated
3 tablespoons salad oil
1 1/2 tablespoons lemon juice
1/2 teaspoon salt
2 tablespoons light cream
1 small onion, chopped fine
1 tablespoon parsley, chopped

Scrub beets thoroughly under running water. Peel and grate beets finely. Combine with apple in a medium-sized salad bowl. Beat oil, lemon juice, and salt with a fork until thick. Stir in cream, chopped onion and parsley. Pour over salad and toss well.

German-Style Coleslaw

1 medium-sized head white cabbage
2 slices bacon, diced
1/2 cup water
1 1/2 tablespoons salad oil
1 1/2 tablespoons vinegar
1/2 teaspoon salt
1 teaspoon parsley, chopped fine

Remove coarse outer leaves from cabbage and cut head into quarters. Remove the core. Shred cabbage very fine and wash thoroughly. Fry bacon in a large pot. Add shredded cabbage and continue to cook for 5 minutes, stirring constantly. Add water and simmer until cabbage is just tender. Combine salad oil, vinegar, salt, and parsley and pour over warm cabbage. Cool before serving.

Strawberry Pretzel Salad

1 stick butter, melted
1 1/4 cups sugar, divided
1 1/2 cups crushed pretzels
1 8-oz. package cream cheese
1 8-oz. container non-dairy 1
   whipped topping
2 packages strawberry gelatin
2 10-oz. packages frozen
   strawberries

Mix butter, 1/4 cup sugar, and pretzels. Spread in a 9x13-inch pan. Bake at 350° for 10 to 15 minutes. Let cool completely. Mix cream cheese, 1 cup of the sugar, and whipped topping. Spread on baked pretzel crust. Mix gelatin, 1 1/2 cups boiling water and strawberries. Let mixture thicken slightly and spread on top. Refrigerate until set.

Bean Salad

1 pound beans	1/4 cup oil
1/2 teaspoon salt	1/4 cup vinegar

Soak beans overnight in cold water. Cook until soft; drain. Beat salt, oil, and vinegar with fork until well blended. Pour over beans while warm. Let stand 1 to 2 hours before serving. Toss salad and serve. Serves six.

Watercress Salad

1 bunch watercress	1/4 cup oil
salt to taste	1/4 cup vinegar or lemon juice

Clean and wash watercress, cut stems and drain thoroughly. Salt the watercress. Mix oil and vinegar, pour over watercress and toss.

Carrot Salad

6 medium-size carrots, shredded	1/2 cup chopped celery
2 apples, cored and diced	fresh ground pepper
1/2 cup raisins	mayonnaise for moisture

Combine all ingredients thoroughly; chill and serve.

Celery Salad

2 large stalks celery	salt and pepper to taste
3 tablespoons vinegar	several strips of bacon, chopped
1 cup beef stock	and fried, along with the fat
1 small onion, chopped	

Scrape celery and boil in salted water until tender. Remove celery and chop. Combine beef stock, onion and salt and pepper; add to celery and mix well. Let stand several hours. Add bacon and bacon drippings; toss and serve. Serves four.

Woolen Mill, 1960s.

Clock from the Amana Furniture Shop.

Photos by Joan Liffring-Zug

The Schanz family, 1970.
Three generations of woodworkers, Schanz Furniture and Refinishing.

Vegetables and Side Dishes

Green Beans with Bacon and Onions
Elsie Oehler

2 pounds green beans
8 slices bacon, chopped

1/2 medium-size onion, chopped
1 1/2 cups water

Wash beans and snip off ends. Leave beans whole or cut into pieces. In saucepan or skillet, over moderate heat, cook bacon and onions until bacon is almost crisp. Drain excess grease and add water and beans. Cover tightly and cook about 30 minutes, stirring occasionally. Add a little more water if the beans should cook dry. Add salt to taste before serving. Serves four.

Pickled Beets
Brick Haus Restaurant

1 1-pound can tiny whole beets
beet liquid from can
1/2 cup sugar

10 tablespoons vinegar
1/2 teaspoon salt

Combine beet liquid, sugar, vinegar, and salt. Add beets. Bring to a boil and let simmer 3 minutes. Refrigerate for one day to two weeks. Serves four.
Note: If tiny beets are not available, cut larger beets into quarters.

Pickled Red Cabbage
Ronneburg Restaurant

1 head red cabbage
2 cups vinegar

2 cups water
2 cups sugar

Shred red cabbage, sprinkle with salt, and place in bowl. Combine vinegar, water, and sugar in pan and bring to boil. Pour hot liquid over cabbage and refrigerate at least 24 hours. Will keep in refrigerator at least a week. This is easy and fast to make, and good. Serves six to eight.

Village scene, 1972.

Photo by Joan Liffring-Zug

Red Cabbage with Apples
Elsie Oehler

2 tablespoons chopped onion
1/2 medium-size red apple,
  chopped

1 tablespoon lard
1 1-pound can sweet-and-sour
  red cabbage

Sauté onion and apple in lard until onion is transparent. Add red cabbage and simmer 20 to 30 minutes. This is best if made a day ahead and reheated. Serves three to four.

Fried Green Tomatoes
Madeline Schuerer Schulte

4 green tomatoes, thickly sliced
2 eggs, beaten
1/2 cup yellow corn meal

1/4 teaspoon salt
black pepper
1/3 cup shortening

Dip the tomato slices in the beaten eggs. Combine corn meal, salt and pepper and dip egg-coated tomatoes in mixture. In a heavy skillet, heat shortening and sauté tomato slices quickly until brown on both sides. Serves four.

Above: Two women working outside a community kitchen.
Below: View of Amana with kitchen gardens, early 1900s.

Green Noodles with Tomatoes
Elsie Oehler

Often, as I purchase spinach noodles in a store, I have someone ask me, "What do you do with those?" Being green in appearance, they do attract attention at the checkout counter. Here is a good recipe to use if you are tempted to try them sometime.

1 8-oz. package spinach noodles
1 16-oz. can tomatoes, cut into
    bite-sized pieces
1 teaspoon salt
1 teaspoon sugar
1/4 teaspoon chervil
1/4 teaspoon marjoram

1/4 teaspoon dill weed
1/2 cup chopped green pepper
3/4 cup chopped onion
3 tablespoons oil or butter
4 slices sharp American cheese
3/4 cup dry bread crumbs
4 tablespoons butter

Cook noodles according to package directions. Drain. Mix tomatoes, salt, sugar, and herbs. Sauté green pepper and onion in oil until tender. Add to tomato mixture and toss with noodles. Place half of mixture in greased 2-quart casserole. Cover with cheese slices. Top with remaining mixture. Lightly sauté bread crumbs in butter and sprinkle over casserole. Bake at 350° for 30 minutes or until bubbly and brown. Serves six.

Honeyed Carrots
Brick Haus Restaurant

1/2 teaspoon salt
1 cup water
12 medium-size carrots, sliced

1/3 cup honey
2 tablespoons vegetable oil
1 teaspoon lemon juice

In a medium saucepan, bring salt and water to a boil. Add carrots. Heat to a boil, then reduce heat. Cover and cook until tender, 10 to 12 minutes. Drain. Cook and stir remaining ingredients in a 10-inch skillet until bubbly. Add carrots. Cook uncovered over low heat, stirring until all carrots are glazed. Serves six.

Baked Potato Casserole
Linda Schuerer

3 tablespoons butter
3 tablespoons flour
1 teaspoon salt
3/4 teaspoon dry mustard
1/4 teaspoon pepper
1 1/2 cups milk

3/4 cup mayonnaise
6 medium-size potatoes, cooked,
   peeled, diced
1 medium-size onion, chopped
6 frankfurters, sliced
1/4 cup buttered bread crumbs

In a small saucepan, melt butter, then blend in flour, salt, mustard, and pepper. Add milk and stir over medium heat until mixture thickens. Boil 1 minute. Remove from heat. Blend in mayonnaise. Fold in potatoes, onions, and frankfurters. Spoon into a 2-quart casserole dish, sprinkle with crumbs and bake at 350° for 30 to 40 minutes. Serves six to eight.

Homemade Noodles
Brick Haus Restaurant

1 1/2 cups flour
1/2 teaspoon salt
1 teaspoon baking powder

3 eggs
3 tablespoons heavy cream
chicken broth, boiling

In a bowl, sift flour, salt and baking powder. Make a well in the center and add eggs and cream. Stir with fork to make a dough. Cover and let stand for 10 minutes, then knead until smooth. Roll dough out on a lightly floured board until very thin. Cover with a cloth and let stand for 30 minutes. Roll dough up from long side and cut into half-inch pieces. Unroll noodles and allow to dry at least 2 hours. Boil noodles in kettle of boiling chicken broth for 8 minutes. Serve the noodles with the broth. Makes 1/2 pound of noodles; serves eight.

Sauerkraut
Herb Hays, Amana Heritage Society Member

3 gallons white cabbage, shredded
12 1-quart canning jars
12 teaspoons salt + 2 tablespoons
12 teaspoons sugar
caraway seed (optional)
boiling water to fill jars

Chop or shred enough white cabbage to fill a 3-gallon container. Do not use the outer leaves or the heart. A kraut cutter, meat slicer or a sharp heavy knife and a board will do. Sterilize 12 quart jars and lids with rubber gaskets. Fill jars with shredded cabbage, packing down gently. Add 1 teaspoon salt and 1 teaspoon sugar to each jar. Also, a sprinkling of caraway seed may be added if desired. Add boiling water to within 1/2-inch of the top of jars. Put the lids on loosely and place in a warm place for five days. Since you will be making the *Sauerkraut* in the summer, an un-airconditioned location such as the garage will be fine. Place the jars in a shallow pan or on a tray as they might run over.

On the fifth day, remove the lids. Press the cabbage down in the jars; it will have floated to the top. Fill the jars to the top with a hot solution of 2 tablespoons salt to a quart of water.

Screw the tops on tightly to seal, and store in a cool dry place. Resist the temptation to open the first jar for at least a month. It really is best to eat in the winter, baked with pork.

Potato Pancakes
Florence Rettig Schuerer

2 1/2 medium-size potatoes,
    peeled, grated and
    drained of liquid
1 teaspoon salt
2 eggs, lightly beaten
1 1/2 teaspoons flour
1/3 cup shortening
applesauce

Toss the potatoes with salt, eggs and flour. Heat the shortening in a heavy skillet and drop in spoonfuls of the potato mixture. Fry until golden brown, turn and fry other side. Serve hot with applesauce. Serves two.

Beer Batter for Vegetables
Elsie Oehler

1 1/4 cups beer (let stand at least one hour to "flatten")
2 tablespoons grated Parmesan cheese
1 tablespoon chopped parsley
1 teaspoon salt

1 1/2 cups flour
1 tablespoon olive oil
1 clove garlic, minced
2 eggs, separated
assorted vegetables for frying
oil for deep-frying

Combine all ingredients except egg whites. Stir well and blend. Beat egg whites until stiff and fold into batter. Dip strips of vegetables such as green pepper, onions, sliced zucchini and thin-sliced cauliflower into batter. Fry in oil at 375° until lightly browned.

Potatoes with Buttered Crumbs
Elsie Oehler

1 quart sliced potatoes
1 tablespoon butter

1 tablespoon shortening
1/2 cup dry bread crumbs

Peel and slice potatoes as for French fries; boil until tender. Fry crumbs in butter and shortening until golden brown. Drain potatoes and toss with crumbs until well-coated. Serves four to six.

Onion Cake
Carol Schuerer Zuber, Barn Restaurant

6 large onions, slivered
1 tablespoon butter
salt and pepper to taste
1 egg, beaten

1-pound package frozen bread dough
1/2 pound bacon, cooked and crumbled

Sauté onions in the butter until limp. Season with salt and pepper. Mix in the egg. Press bread dough into the bottom of a 9-inch square baking dish. Pour the onion mixture over the dough and sprinkle with bacon. Bake at 400° for 30 minutes. Serve warm. Serves six.

Peas and Carrots

1 pound small carrots
2 tablespoons butter
1/2 cup water
1 8-oz. can tiny peas, drained

1 teaspoon salt
1 teaspoon sugar
1 tablespoon chopped parsley

Peel carrots. If they are small, leave whole, if not, cut into 3-inch pieces. Melt butter in saucepan and add carrots, stirring until they are coated. Add water and cook 10 to 15 minutes, or until tender. Add peas and heat through. Season with salt and sugar. Sprinkle with parsley; serve.

Asparagus with Ham and Pancakes

2 to 3 pounds fresh asparagus
1 1/2 teaspoons salt, divided
2 tablespoons sugar
2 1/2 cups flour

2 eggs
milk as needed
1/2 pound smoked ham, sliced
4 tablespoons melted butter

Trim asparagus, cutting off woody ends. Cook asparagus upright in a steamer with 1/2 cup boiling water, or in a flat pan cover asparagus with boiling water. Add 1 teaspoon of salt and the 2 tablespoons of sugar to cooking water. Cook 12 to 20 minutes, depending on size and tenderness. Remove and drain. Combine flour, eggs, 1/2 teaspoon of salt, and enough milk to make a thin pancake batter. Fry pancakes in a hot skillet and reserve. When asparagus is tender, remove from pot and wrap 1 to 2 stalks in a pancake. Place rolled pancakes on a platter with the sliced ham. Pour melted butter over pancakes and serve.

Sautéed Cucumbers

2 cucumbers
3 tablespoons butter
1 teaspoon salt
1 tablespoon sugar

1 teaspoon pepper
1 1/2 tablespoons vinegar
2 tablespoons flour
1 cup dill, finely chopped

Pare, seed and dice cucumbers. Melt butter in a skillet. Add cucumber, salt, sugar, pepper, and vinegar and cook over medium heat for 20 minutes. Sprinkle with flour, stirring to thicken. Add dill before serving.

Kohlrabi

8 kohlrabies
2 teaspoons salt
large pinch of baking soda
4 tablespoons butter
2 tablespoons flour

2 cups beef stock
salt, pepper and nutmeg to taste
2 tablespoons parsley, chopped
4 tablespoons cream

Remove tender leaves from bulb and cook in salted water with a small amount of baking soda until tender. Rinse well in cold water; drain and chop finely. Set aside. Pare and slice the kohlrabies; cook in lightly salted water until done, about 1/2 hour. Prepare a light sauce from butter, flour, beef stock, seasonings, and cream. Add sliced kohlrabi and bring to a boil again. The chopped cooked greens can be added to the sliced kohlrabi, or can be served separately. Serves eight.

Stuffed Cabbage Rolls

2/3 cup uncooked wild rice
1 head of white cabbage
2 pounds ground beef
1 pound pork sausage

1 teaspoon ground cloves
2 teaspoons cinnamon
salt to taste

Cook rice according to package directions. Core the cabbage. Start cooking cabbage with top of head up, then switch the top down so the thickest part gets more steaming. Cook until leaves are pliable and can be removed from head without breaking. Remove cabbage to a large platter. Pull leaves apart carefully; cool. Mix cooked rice, ground beef, sausage and spices together. Form into thick cylindrical patties. Roll in 2 cabbage leaves placed on top of each other. Place rolls in a small, flat roaster. Add some water to the pan and cover. Bake at 350° for an hour or more, until tops of rolls are brown and meats are cooked. Check occasionally during baking and baste if leaves are drying. Serve on platter with pan juices. Cabbage rolls reheat well and also may be frozen.

Amana Wines

Many of the brick and sandstone houses in the seven Amana villages are adorned with white trellises upon which Concord grape vines are climbing.

People harvest these grapes to make grape juice, jelly and home-made wine. Many gardeners grow rhubarb in their back yards to use for pies, cobblers, jams and wine.

Grape and rhubarb wines are the traditional wines of Amana and can be bought in all of the wineries. The wineries buy their fruits in great quantities and do not reap them from the home trellises.

Critic Grape by William Prestele. A Prestele exhibition is in the Museum of Amana History.

In the days of communal life, before 1932, wine was made for the entire community. A *Weinmeister* (vineyard overseer) was in charge of grape growing. He appointed each family to care for rows of grapes. At harvest time, the grapes were hauled to the press house and made into wine.

Under the communal system adults received punchable tickets for their allotment of wine. Men were allowed twenty gallons per year and women twelve per year. Not everyone used this generous allotment.

Liebesmahl wein, for communal services in church, was made and stored separately.

Rhubarb wine was typically made "on the sly." People wishing to make and store their own few gallons would crush rhubarb stalks and make the juice into wine in their basements.

When the national Prohibition Amendment went into effect in 1919, a total of 19,000 gallons of wine was poured into the drainage ditches of Amana. The story is still told that on the next morning, every catfish between Amana and New Orleans was pleading for aspirin.

Fruit press and wagon wheel,
Cooper Shop Museum, Middle Amana, 1970s.

Recipes with Wine

Wine Dainties
Elsie Mattes, Sandstone Winery

1/2 cup butter or margarine	1/4 teaspoon salt
1 1/2 cups sugar	1/2 teaspoon baking soda
2 eggs	1/2 teaspoon baking powder
1/2 cup sweet Concord	1 cup raisins
grape wine	1 cup chopped nuts
2 1/2 cups sifted flour	

Cream butter and sugar thoroughly. Add eggs and wine and beat well. Sift flour, salt, soda, and baking powder together and add to egg mixture. Work in raisins and nuts. Drop from teaspoon onto greased cookie sheets and bake 15 minutes at 350°. Makes three to four dozen.

Water Cake with Wine Sauce
Helen Kraus

Cake:

2 cups sugar	2 cups all-purpose flour
4 eggs	2 teaspoons baking powder
1 cup hot water	

Beat sugar and eggs together until well blended and fluffy. Add hot water. Sift together flour and baking powder; add gradually to sugar, egg and water mixture, blend well. Bake in greased and floured 13x9-inch pan at 350° for 30 to 25 minutes.

Wine Sauce:

1 cup water, divided	1/4 cup sugar
2 tablespoons flour or 1 1/2	1 cup Concord grape wine
tablespoons cornstarch	

Bring 3/4 cup of water to boil. Add flour or cornstarch which has been blended with 1/4 cup of water. Cook until clear and thickened. Add sugar and cook a few minutes longer. Remove from heat and add wine. Cool. Pour over cake and serve immediately.

Photo by Dr. Christian Herrmann

Photo by F.W. Miller

Above: Fishing in the Iowa River, circa 1900.
Below: Men fishing near the Indian Dam, a prehistoric fish weir.

Rabbit with Tarragon
Helen Kraus

1 young rabbit
1/4 cup flour
1 teaspoon salt
1/4 teaspoon pepper

4 to 6 tablespoons butter
1 cup dry rhubarb wine, divided
1/4 cup fresh tarragon, or
   1 teaspoon dried tarragon

Skin and clean rabbit, reserving liver. Cut into serving pieces. Combine flour with salt and pepper. Dredge rabbit pieces in seasoned flour. Melt butter in large skillet and brown rabbit quickly on all sides, being careful that butter does not burn. Lower heat and add 3/4 cup dry rhubarb wine. Cover and simmer gently about 45 minutes, or until rabbit is tender. Soak tarragon in 1/4 cup dry rhubarb wine for 30 minutes and add mixture to skillet. Increase heat and turn pieces of rabbit. Cook five minutes. Remove rabbit to heated platter. Pour sauce over to serve. Liver may be sautéed in butter 5 minutes, minced, and added to the sauce just at serving time. A delightful way to prepare rabbit—top-of-the-stove *Hasenpfeffer*. Serves four.

Baked Fish
Helen Kraus

1/2 cup chopped celery
1 1/2 pounds catfish
   fillets (or any other fish
   fillets), fresh or frozen
3/4 teaspoon salt
1/4 teaspoon crushed rosemary

1/4 teaspoon pepper
1/4 teaspoon paprika
1 medium-sized tomato, sliced
1/2 cup chopped green onion
1/4 cup dry rhubarb wine

Layer celery into shallow baking pan. Arrange fish over celery, slightly overlapping fillets. Sprinkle with seasonings, top with tomato and onion. Add wine. Bake at 350° for 25 minutes or until fish is flaky. Serves four.

Editor's note: For many years Helen and George Kraus had their own winery in Middle Amana. The recipes credited to them come from their book, The Story of an Amana Winemaker.

Pork Loin Roast
Helen Kraus

1 4-pound pork loin roast
8 prunes, pitted and chopped
1 tart apple, cored and diced
1 teaspoon seasoning salt
1/4 teaspoon ginger
1/4 teaspoon pepper
1/8 teaspoon garlic powder

1 tablespoon flour
1/2 cup rhubarb wine
flour
1/4 cup water
1 small jar currant jelly
1/8 teaspoon garlic powder
salt and pepper

Make a hole through center of loin (better yet, ask the butcher to do it) and stuff with prunes and apple. Combine seasoning salt, ginger, pepper and garlic powder; press to coat the roast. Dust roast with flour and place in roaster. Pour wine into bottom of pan and roast 2 hours at 400°. Pour off drippings and thicken with flour stirred into water. Stir in jelly and garlic powder. Salt and pepper the gravy to taste. Serves four.

Marinated Beef Roast
Helen Kraus

1 2-pound beef roast
3/4 cup soy sauce
1 cup tomato wine
1/2 cup honey
1/4 teaspoon oregano

2 garlic cloves, crushed
1 teaspoon basil
1 teaspoon seasoned salt
1/2 teaspoon pepper
2 slices ginger root

Combine all liquids and seasonings and pour half of it over roast. Marinate 3 to 4 hours. Add remaining liquid when roast goes into oven. Bake 1 hour at 375°. Serves four.

French Herbed Chicken
Helen Kraus

1 3-pound broiler-fryer
   chicken, cut up
1 tablespoon shortening
1 8-oz. can (1 cup) small
   onions, drained
1/2 cup coarsely
   chopped carrot

1 clove garlic, crushed
2 tablespoons snipped parsley
1/4 teaspoon crushed thyme
1 2-oz. can sliced mushrooms
1 cup dry rhubarb wine
2 or 3 stalks celery, cut up
1 medium-sized bay leaf

Brown chicken in hot fat in skillet. Season with salt and pepper, if desired, and place in a 2-quart casserole. Drain excess fat from skillet; add remaining ingredients except celery and bay leaf. Heat, scraping up browned pieces. Pour over chicken. Tuck in celery pieces and bay leaf. Cover and bake at 350° for 1 1/4 hours. Remove bay leaf and celery and serve. Serves four.

Orange-Pineapple Chicken
Helen Kraus

1 broiler-fryer chicken, cut up
1/4 cup biscuit baking mix
1 teaspoon monosodium glutamate
1/2 teaspoon salt
1/4 teaspoon basil
1/4 teaspoon sage
1/4 cup corn oil

1/2 cup frozen orange juice
   concentrate
1/4 cup pineapple juice
3 tablespoons brown sugar
2 tablespoons dry rhubarb wine
1 teaspoon prepared mustard
1/3 teaspoon ground ginger

Mix together baking mix, monosodium glutamate, salt, basil, and sage. Coat chicken pieces. Heat corn oil in frying pan over medium heat. Add chicken and brown on all sides; place in foil-lined baking pan. Mix together juices, brown sugar, wine, mustard, and ginger. Brush on chicken every 15 minutes while cooking. Bake in 325° oven, uncovered, for about 1 hour or until fork can be inserted with ease. Can be garnished with pineapple slices, orange wedges, and parsley. Serves four.

Marinated Round Steak
Alma Ehrle, Ehrle Brothers Winery

1 round steak (one slab cut 1/2 inch thick)	1 onion, minced or in rings
flour	salt and pepper to taste
	1 cup *piestengel* (dry rhubarb wine)

Pound flour into steak (Mrs. Ehrle uses the edge of a saucer) on both sides. Brown in skillet. Remove steak from skillet and cut into pieces of serving size. Place a layer of meat pieces into the same skillet (if oven proof) or a casserole dish. Top meat with layers of onions and season as desired. Repeat layer of meat and onions. Add the cup of *piestengel.* Put lid on skillet and bake at 350° for 1 1/2 hours. More wine may be added if steak gets too dry.

Wild Duck in Wine
Carl and Fern Oehl, Colony Market Place Restaurant

1 wild duck, dressed	1 onion, diced fine
salt, pepper, paprika	4 carrots, diced
flour	several sprigs of parsley
1/4 pound butter	2 whole cloves
1 cup soup stock or consommé	3 bay leaves
	4 peppercorns, slightly crushed
juice of one lemon	1/2 cup claret or Burgundy

Cut duck into sections similar to chicken, as for frying. Wipe bird dry and season with salt, pepper and paprika. Dredge in flour. In a Dutch oven, brown the duck in butter. Add remaining ingredients except wine. Cover and cook on low heat until tender. Add wine during cooking. If necessary, add a little water while cooking to keep moist. Do not cover the entire bird with liquid.

German Peasant Stew
Helen Kraus

2 tablespoons oil
1 cup sliced onion
1 clove garlic, crushed
3 pounds stewing beef,
    cut in 1-inch cubes
8 1/2 cups beef broth
1/2 cup Concord grape wine
1 tablespoon sugar
1 teaspoon salt

1 bay leaf
1 1/2 pounds potatoes, peeled
    and cubed (4 cups)
2 cups sliced carrots
1 teaspoon dill weed
1 tablespoon flour
1/2 cup Concord grape wine
    (optional)

In a large stewing pot or large electric skillet, heat oil and add onion and garlic. Sauté just until tender, not browned. Remove and set aside. Add half of beef, brown on all sides, and remove. Brown remaining beef. Return beef and onions to pot. Stir in broth, 1/2 cup wine, sugar, salt and bay leaf. Reduce heat. Cover and simmer until meat is tender, 1 1/2 to 2 hours. Add potatoes, carrots and dill. Simmer until vegetables are tender, 20 to 30 minutes. Mix flour with a little water and stir into broth. Cook and stir until thickened. Remaining wine may be added at this time for stronger wine flavor in the gravy. Serves six.

Community kitchen workers, 1900s.

Roast Pheasant with Apples and Kraut

1 1/2- to 2-pound pheasant
2 quarts water
1 teaspoon salt
1 tablespoon vinegar
1 1/2 tablespoons flour
2 tablespoons butter
3 cups sauerkraut

1/2 teaspoon minced onion
2 tablespoons brown sugar
caraway seed
1/4 cup water
2 medium-sized tart apples
    unpeeled and cut into wedges
2 tablespoons white wine

Clean pheasant and pin. Soak in solution of water, salt, and vinegar for 2 hours to remove bloods and to sweeten. Cut into serving pieces. Dredge in flour and brown in butter for fifteen minutes. Remove from skillet and blend into drippings. Add sauerkraut, onion, brown sugar, and seasonings. Turn into 10-cut casserole or roaster. Arrange pheasant pieces on top of sauerkraut. Add water; cover and bake in a 350° oven for forty-five minutes. Cut apples into wedges, core and arrange around pheasant. Pour wine over all; cover and return to oven and bake an additional twenty-five minutes or until tender. Garnish with fresh parsley.

*Mesquakie Indians from Tama, Iowa, frequently
visited the Amana Colonies in the early 1900s.*

Wine Sauce for Ham
Helen Kraus

1 can cherry pie filling
1/3 cup brown sugar
1/3 to 1 cup sweet cherry wine

1/2 cup raisins
1 teaspoon prepared mustard
1 cup currant or apple jelly

Mix all ingredients and heat thoroughly. Spoon over ham every 20 minutes as ham cooks. Serve remainder with meal.

Marinated Precooked Ham
Alma Ehrle, Ehrle Brothers Winery

3 to 4-pound precooked ham   1 1/2 cups dry grape wine

Put ham in roaster. Add the wine. Bake at 325° for 1 1/2 hours. Baste occasionally. When ham is done, slice and place on serving platter; pour the wine sauce over the ham. If leftover ham is reheated, add wine when reheating.

Fruit Compote Deluxe
Elsie Mattes, Sandstone Winery

4 cups mixed dried fruit
1 21-oz. can cherry pie filling
1 apple, chopped
2 cups water

1/3 cup cherry brandy
1/2 cup dry rhubarb wine
2 tablespoons honey

Combine ingredients in a crock pot. Cover and cook on low for 6 hours. Serve hot or cold.

Wine barrel in Amana.

Red Cabbage in Wine
Helen Kraus

1/2 cup butter or margarine
4 pounds red cabbage, shredded
1 cup Concord grape wine
2 cups sliced apples

pinch of ground cloves
1 tablespoon sugar
grated peel of 1 lemon

Melt butter or margarine in a large, heavy skillet over low heat. Add cabbage and stir while cooking until cabbage is softened and limp. Add wine and apples and stir to mix well. Cover tightly and cook until cabbage and apples are tender. Add cloves, sugar, and lemon peel and cook 3 minutes more. Serves six.

Oma's Beets
Helen Kraus

1 8-oz. can small whole beets
1 teaspoon cornstarch
1/4 cup red beet juice or sweet
    Concord grape wine

1 1/2 teaspoons butter
salt and pepper

Drain beets, reserving 1/4 cup of liquid. Thinly slice beets and set aside. In a saucepan, gradually stir reserved liquid into cornstarch until smooth, then add the wine. Cook over medium heat, stirring constantly, until sauce is clear and thick. Stir in butter and beets and reheat. Add salt and pepper to taste. A nice way to dress up an often neglected and overlooked vegetable. Serves two or three.

Community kitchen gardeners planting onion sets, High Amana, 1908.

Wine Jelly
Helen Kraus

3 cups sugar
2 cups wine

1/2 of a 6-oz. bottle of liquid
fruit pectin

Measure sugar and wine into the top of a double boiler and mix well. Place over but not touching boiling water. Stir until sugar is dissolved, 3 to 4 minutes. Remove from heat and quickly stir in fruit pectin, mixing well. Quickly pour hot jelly into sterilized jars. When jelly is firm, cover with melted paraffin.

Wine Cherry Pancakes
Helen Kraus

A delightful switch with tart cherries in soft, delicate cakes.

4 medium-sized French
  bread rolls
1 teaspoon ground cinnamon
1/2 cup sugar
2 eggs
1/4 cup sifted all-purpose flour
2 teaspoons sugar
1/2 teaspoon salt

1/2 cup milk
1/2 cup cherry wine
1 1-pound can tart pitted red
  cherries, drained
5 tablespoons butter, softened
  and whipped

Soak rolls in water to cover. Stir cinnamon and 1/2 cup sugar together and set aside. In a mixing bowl, beat eggs until light. Add flour, 2 teaspoons sugar, salt, milk, and wine and beat until smooth. Squeeze rolls dry and crumble into batter. Fold in drained cherries. Drop batter onto medium-hot griddle in mounds 1 1/2 inches in diameter and bake until crisp and brown on one side. Carefully turn and brown other side. Serve hot with a dollop of whipped butter, and sprinkle with cinnamon and sugar mixture. Makes 30 to 36 little cakes.

Jellies, Jams, and Pickles

Rhubarb Marmalade
Ruth Schmieder

1 pound rhubarb, cut into
    3/4-inch pieces

1 cup crushed pineapple
3 cups sugar

In a saucepan, mix all ingredients and boil rapidly for 25 or 30 minutes until thick. Put in sterile jars and seal when cool.

Peach Jam
Henrietta Moershel Ruff

"My recipe for peach jam, as my mother gave it to me, reads, 'Use equal weight of sugar and pulp. Start low, then cook fast for twenty minutes.' That's all! It's enough for me, because I grew up with jam cooked like that—strawberries, cherries, peaches, plums, apricots, etc. I don't know if it's an Amana recipe, but it's a family one. Perhaps other Amana homemakers use it, too."

Peaches should be peeled and cut fine. Use equal weight of sugar and pulp. Best results are obtained if not more than 3 pounds of fruit is cooked at a time. Use a large, deep kettle so jam does not boil over. Start low till sugar is dissolved and well-mixed with fruit, stirring frequently. Then cook rapidly for 20 minutes, stirring occasionally so jam doesn't stick. Let cool somewhat, stirring frequently, so that the fruit absorbs the liquid. Pour into hot sterilized glasses and seal with paraffin. Jam may be frozen; in that case, use screw-top jars and lids, no paraffin.

Other fruit may be used: strawberries, whole or cut up; raspberries; blackberries; pitted cherries; pears, chopped or coarsely grated, with some lemon juice and finely cut rind added; ground cherries, also with lemon juice and rind; apricots and plums, chopped, peeled, or unpeeled.

Dandelion Jelly
Helen Kraus

What could be more pleasant than picking the bright yellow blossoms on a sunny, summer morning to make jelly to sweeten breakfast on frosty winter mornings? Even if only a few dandelions can be found, a few are enough to make jelly. Directions are simple and easy.

1 quart dandelion blossoms	1 teaspoon lemon or
1 quart water	orange extract
1 package pectin	4 1/2 cups sugar

In the morning, while the sun is shining to open blossoms fully, pick one quart of blossoms—no stems, just blossoms. Boil blossoms in water for 3 minutes. Strain 3 cups of liquid; discard blossoms. To the strained liquid, add pectin, lemon or orange extract, and sugar. Boil 3 more minutes. Pour into sterilized jars. When jelly is firm, seal with paraffin. It is so light and lovely, it resembles the taste of honey.

Photograph by Joan Liffring-Zug

Amana children picking dandelions, 1980s.

Zucchini Jam

6 cups grated fresh zucchini
water
6 cups sugar

2 3-oz. packages lemon gelatin
1 cup crushed pineapple
1/2 cup lemon juice

Boil zucchini in water until it looks transparent; drain. Add sugar, gelatin, pineapple, and juice. Mix well and return to heat; boil for 5 minutes. Pour into sterilized jars and seal. When cool, store in refrigerator.

Bread and Butter Pickles

6 medium-sized cucumbers
3 onions, sliced
1 cup sugar
1 cup vinegar

1/4 teaspoon pepper
1 teaspoon celery seed
1 teaspoon mustard
1/8 teaspoon turmeric

Peel and slice cucumbers. Add sliced onions and let stand in salt water for about 1 hour. Bring sugar, vinegar, pepper, celery seed, mustard and turmeric to a boil; boil for about 1 minute. Add cucumbers and onions. Heat thoroughly and pack in jars while hot; seal. Yields 3 to 4 pints.

Watermelon Pickles

rinds from watermelon,
   cut into pieces

3 1/2 cups water
1/2 cup salt

Syrup:
1 quart cider vinegar
3 pounds sugar

1 teaspoon whole cloves
2 tablespoons crushed
   stick cinnamon

Soak rinds, scraped clean, in the water and salt overnight. Drain. In a saucepan cover rinds with fresh water and cook until tender. Drain. For the syrup combine vinegar and sugar in a saucepan. Add cloves and cinnamon. Bring mixture to boiling until sugar is dissolved. Add the watermelon rinds and cook for 15 minutes. Put in sterile jars and seal.

Village barber, early 1900s.

Horseradish

2/3 cup diced, fresh horseradish   1/2 cup vinegar
1/2 cup water   1 teaspoon lemon juice

Grind all ingredients in a blender until finely grated. More water and vinegar may need to be added in equal parts to help mixture "flow." Store in refrigerator. Horseradish loses its kick after about 5 weeks, so it should be made in small batches.

Variation: Beetroot and Horseradish Relish

1 cup diced, cold cooked beetroot   2 tablespoons vinegar
3 tablespoons grated horseradish   1/2 teaspoon salt
2 teaspoons sugar

Mix beetroot, horseradish, sugar, vinegar, and salt together. Store in jars and serve with cold meat and fish.

Remembering the Amanas

Springtime in Middle Amana. Photo by Joan Liffring-Zug, 1970s
Before the Great Change in 1932, buildings in Amana were not painted.

"*The Amanas Yesterday* book gave me a lovely nostalgic trip. This was the Amanas as remembered in my early youth, before 1918, unpainted, unimproved, and noncommercial. The road then led down through Swisher, Cou Falls, and along the river road to East Amana. We went in the Peerless Touring Car or with my Grandmother Cook or Aunt Ella Smith in their chauffeur-driven cars. We would stop at Hi Zimmermann's. He was careful not to bring out the wine when my grandmother or aunt were along as they were WCTU'rs (Women's Christian Temperance Union), then on to the woolen mill and the general store for shopping, past the lily pond, Middle, High, West, Lower South and end up for dinner at the Zerold's in Upper South by the bakery. The food was really family-style then. I don't believe we ordered anything, and we sat at long common tables with whoever happened to be there at the time. The over-all impression was plainness, unpainted drabness, but what a perfect foil for the neatness of the land, the gardens, the arbors, the flowers.

—*Sutherland Cook, Cedar Rapids, Iowa.*
From a letter to Penfield Press publisher Joan Liffring-Zug, 1975.

Breads, Pancakes, Muffins, and Dumplings

Höh Oma's Weihnachts Stollen
(Grandmother's Christmas Yeast Cake)
Rebecca Moershel

4 packages dry yeast
5 pounds flour
1 tablespoon salt
2 1/2 pounds sugar
1 teaspoon nutmeg
2 teaspoons cinnamon
3/4 pound melted butter

1/2 cup candied citron
1 1/2 quarts warm milk
1/2 pound raisins
1/2 teaspoon almond flavoring
2 cups nuts, coarsely chopped
    (almonds, pecans, and
    English walnuts)

Dissolve yeast in lukewarm water. Add 2 cups flour, mix well, then let rise until double in bulk.

Sift remaining flour into large pan together with salt, sugar, nutmeg, and cinnamon. Add yeast, melted butter, citron, and milk to make a medium-stiff dough. Knead thoroughly. Add raisins, flavoring, and nuts and knead again until well blended. Again let rise until double in bulk.

Divide dough into eight parts. Shape each to fit into greased loaf pan and let rise until double in bulk. Just before baking, cut a deep gash down the center of each loaf. Bake in 350° oven for about 50 minutes. When done, brush well with more melted butter and sprinkle with powdered sugar and cinnamon. Makes eight loaves.

Historic view of the Amana Millrace, 1900s.

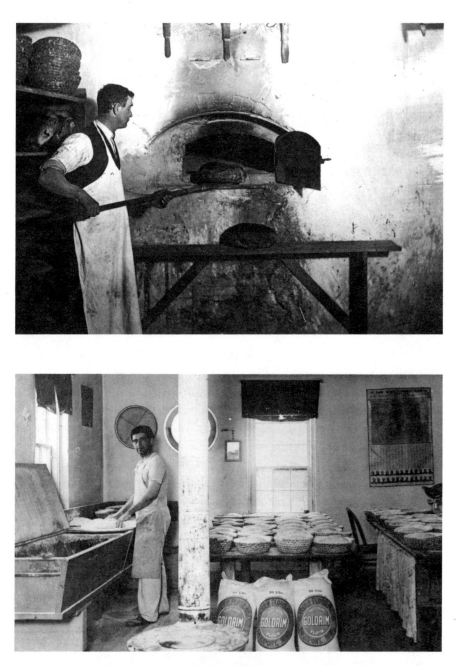

Bread bakers for the community kitchens, early 1900s.

Rye Bread
Madeline Schuerer Schulte

3 packages active dry yeast
1 1/2 cups warm water
1/4 cup molasses
1/3 cup sugar
4 teaspoons salt
3 tablespoons caraway seed

2 3/4 cups rye flour
2 tablespoons shortening
3 1/2 to 4 cups all-purpose flour
1 egg white
2 tablespoons water

Dissolve the yeast in the warm water. Stir in molasses, sugar, salt and caraway seed. Stir in the rye flour until smooth. Work in shortening. Using hands, work in enough of the all-purpose flour to make a dough that is easy to handle. Turn onto a floured board and knead until smooth, about 10 minutes. Place dough in a clean, greased bowl, cover and let rise in a warm place until it doubles in size. Shape dough into two round, slightly flattened loaves. Place far apart on a large, greased baking sheet. Cover with a damp cloth and let rise in a warm place until double in size. Preheat the oven to 375°. Mix the egg white with the water and brush the loaves. Bake 30 to 40 minutes until done. Makes two loaves.

Honey Whole Wheat Bread
Helen Kraus, from Honey Recipes from Amana

2 packages yeast
3 cups lukewarm water, divided
5 cups white flour
4 cups whole wheat flour

1 tablespoon salt
3 tablespoons butter
1/2 cup honey

Pour a part of the warm water into a bowl with the yeast. Mix all ingredients together and knead until velvety in texture. Let rise until doubled. Punch down and let rise again. Divide into three parts and place in greased loaf pans. Let rise again until dough is above the edge of the pan. Bake in preheated 375° oven for 30 minutes. Remove from pans and brush top with butter. Return to oven and bake 15 minutes more.

Loaves of Open Hearth Bread baked by Jack Hahn at his bakery in Middle Amana. The bakery is over 100 years old and is open from spring to fall. Featured are white and rye breads, an assortment of coffee cakes and other specialties from recipes passed down through the years. Amana people order Hahn's Ham Baked in Bread for Easter dinner and other special occasions. (Recipe on page 89.)

Yeast Dumplings with Cinnamon Sauce

Dumplings:

1 cup milk

1/2 cup lard

1 tablespoon sugar

1 teaspoon salt

2 eggs, beaten

1/2 cake compressed yeast

1/4 cup warm water

4 cups sifted flour

To Cook:

1 tablespoon lard

3/4 cup boiling water

1 teaspoon salt

To Serve:

2 tablespoons bread crumbs

2 tablespoons butter

Heat milk; add lard, sugar, salt, and beaten eggs. When cooled to luke-warm, add yeast dissolved in warm water. Add flour. Let rise overnight in a warm place.

Form dough into dumplings about 2 inches across and let rise again on cloth-covered board till double in bulk. Into heavy skillet with tight-fitting cover, put lard, boiling water and salt. Place dumplings side by side in skillet; cover and simmer 15 minutes without removing lid. Place in serving dish and top with bread crumbs which have been browned in butter. Serve with cinnamon sauce (see recipe below). Serves six to eight.

Cinnamon Sauce

1/4 cup sugar

4 tablespoons flour

1 tablespoon cinnamon

1/2 cup cold milk

3 1/2 cups scalded milk

Mix sugar, flour and cinnamon. Moisten with cold milk, add to scalded milk, and cook in top of double boiler for 20 minutes. Serve hot with Yeast Dumplings.

Apple Muffins
Brick Haus Restaurant

1 egg, beaten
1/4 cup shortening, melted
1/2 cup sugar
2 1/2 cups finely chopped, cored
    and peeled apples,
2 cups all-purpose flour
1 tablespoon + 1 teaspoon
    baking powder

1/2 teaspoon salt
1/2 teaspoon ground cinnamon
1/8 teaspoon ground nutmeg
1 cup milk
1 tablespoon sugar
1/2 teaspoon ground cinnamon

Combine beaten egg, melted shortening and 1/2 cup sugar, stirring well. Add apples and mix well. Combine flour, baking powder, salt, 1/2 teaspoon cinnamon and nutmeg. Alternating with the milk, add flour mixture to egg mixture, stirring just until moistened. Spoon into greased muffin pans, filling 2/3 full. Combine the 1 tablespoon sugar with 1/2 teaspoon cinnamon and sprinkle over batter. Bake at 375° for 20 to 25 minutes. Makes 15 muffins.

Spring cleaning, early 1900s. Spring cleaning started on the first warm day of the year, and was done one room at a time. Churches, public buildings, shops and stores were always a group effort. Today, the churches of the Community of True Inspiration are still cleaned by the entire congregation.

Oma's Pretzels
Madeline Schuerer Schulte

1 package active dry yeast
1/2 teaspoon sugar
1 1/2 cups warm beer
   (105-115°)

4 1/2 cups all-purpose flour
1 egg, beaten
coarse salt

In a large mixing bowl, dissolve yeast and sugar in warm beer. Add flour and blend well. Turn dough out onto a lightly floured surface. Knead 8 to 10 minutes until dough is smooth and elastic. Place dough in a greased bowl, turning to grease top. Cover and let rise in a warm place (85°) about 1 hour or until double in size. Cut dough into 24 pieces. Roll each piece into a ball. With floured hands, roll each ball between palms to form a rope 14 to 16 inches long. Twist each rope into a pretzel shape. Place on greased baking sheets about 1 1/2 inches apart. Brush each pretzel with egg and sprinkle with coarse salt. Bake at 475° for 12 to 15 minutes until golden brown. Remove pretzels to a wire rack. Serve warm. Makes about 2 dozen.

Potato Bread
Madeline Schuerer Schulte

1 package active dry yeast
1/2 cup lukewarm water
1 cup milk, scalded
2/3 cup sugar

1 teaspoon salt
2 eggs, lightly beaten
1/2 cup mashed potatoes
6 cups flour (approximately)

Dissolve the yeast in the water. Combine the scalded milk, sugar and salt and let stand until lukewarm. Beat the eggs into the mashed potatoes and gradually beat in the cooled milk mixture. Add the dissolved yeast. Stir in enough flour to make a manageable dough. Turn onto a lightly floured board and knead until smooth, about 10 minutes. Place in a clean, greased bowl; cover and let rise until double in size, about 1 hour. Knock dough down and shape into 2 loaves. Place in 2 greased 9x5x3-inch loaf pans. Cover with a damp cloth and let rise in a warm place until double in size. Preheat oven to 375°. Bake 40 minutes or until done. Makes 2 loaves.

Bread Sticks
Madeline Schuerer Schulte

2 packages active dry yeast
1 tablespoon sugar
2 teaspoons salt
1/4 cup shortening
1 1/2 cups warm water, divided
3 to 3 1/2 cups flour, divided

1 egg, beaten with
    1 tablespoon water
coarse salt (optional)
sesame seeds (optional)
poppy seeds (optional)

In a large mixing bowl, combine yeast, sugar and salt. Add the shortening and 1/4 cup of the water. Using a wooden spoon, beat mixture well for about 3 minutes. Add 1/2 cup of the flour and continue beating. Alternately add flour (1 cup at a time) and water until a soft dough forms. Reserve 1/2 cup flour for kneading. Place dough on a floured surface and knead for several minutes until dough springs back when pressed with a finger. Dough must be smooth and all flour absorbed from the kneading area. Cover dough with a towel and let it rise about 5 minutes. Then shape into a roll about 20 to 22 inches long. With a sharp knife, cut it into 20 to 25 pieces. Using palms of hands, roll out each piece to any size you like. Place sticks on greased baking sheets about 1 inch apart. Brush each stick lightly with the egg-and-water mixture, then sprinkle with coarse salt, sesame seeds, or poppy seeds if desired. Let sit about 20 minutes, barely rising. Bake at 300° for about 30 minutes until light brown. Makes twenty to twenty-five breadsticks.

Amana Society bread truck, 1930s.

Rhubarb Bread

2 1/2 cups + 2 tablespoons flour
1 1/2 cups dark brown sugar
1 teaspoon baking soda
1/2 teaspoon salt
1 egg

1 cup buttermilk
1/2 cup corn oil
1 teaspoon vanilla extract
1 cup chopped fresh rhubarb
butter and sugar for topping

In a bowl mix 2 1/2 cups flour, brown sugar, soda and salt. In a separate bowl combine egg, buttermilk, oil and vanilla. Add to dry ingredients and mix well. Toss the rhubarb pieces in the 2 tablespoons flour and fold into batter. Pour into four greased 7x3x2-inch loaf pans; dot with butter and sprinkle with sugar. Bake at 350° for 45 minutes, or until toothpick comes out clean. Cool in pan for fifteen minutes before removing to wire rack.

Meat, Poultry, and Wild Game

Paprika Cream Schnitzel
Brick Haus Restaurant

4 slices bacon
1 1/2 pounds veal cutlets
(cut into individual portions
1/2-inch thick)
2 tablespoons chopped onion

2 tablespoons sweet Hungarian
paprika
salt to taste
1 cup sour cream
1/2 cup tomato sauce

Cook the bacon until crisp. Remove from the skillet, crumble, and reserve. In the bacon drippings, brown the veal, add the onion and cook until lightly browned. Season with the paprika and salt. Stir in the sour cream and the tomato sauce. Cover and simmer for 20 minutes until the veal is tender (do not boil). Sprinkle with the bacon bits. Great when accompanied by egg noodles or rice. Serves four.

German-Style Pickled Ham
Amana Meat Shop and Smokehouse

ham ends and pieces
mixture of water and vinegar

onion slices (optional)
pimiento (optional)

Cut ham into 3/4-inch cubes. Prepare a mixture of 1/2 water and 1/2 vinegar; prepare enough to cover the ham cubes. Add onion and pimiento, if used. Let stand refrigerated overnight. Serve cold.

Colony Inn, 1930s.

Venison Stew
Carl and Fern Oehl, Colony Market Place

1 large onion, chopped
butter
2 to 3 pounds venison,
    cut into cubes

3 cups broth or bouillon
3 to four carrots
3 to 4 medium potatoes
6 stalks celery

Sauté onion in skillet with a little butter. Remove onion, brown venison chunks in skillet. Add onion and cover with broth. Simmer 1 to 1 1/2 hours. Cut vegetables into bite-size pieces; cook separately until almost tender. Mix all ingredients together in large pan or roaster. Season with salt and pepper, or seasoned salt to taste. Simmer over medium heat. Variation: Recipe can also be used for lamb or beef stew. Serves six.

Braised Pheasant
Carl and Fern Oehl

1 whole pheasant
flour seasoned with
    salt and pepper
6 peppercorns
4 whole cloves

3 bay leaves
1 sliced carrot
1 tablespoon lemon juice
1 cup consommé

Cut pheasant into pieces. Soak in salt water 3 hours or overnight. Drain and wipe dry. Dredge in seasoned flour. In a Dutch oven or heavy covered kettle, brown in hot fat. Add remaining ingredients. Cover and simmer 1 1/2 hours or until tender. Watch that the pan does not go dry. Add water or more consommé if necessary. Make gravy from drippings.

Homestead, Iowa.

Flocks of chickens were kept at each community kitchen.

Below: Community Kitchen Museum, Middle Amana.

"It really didn't make so much difference to have the Great Change in 1932. Even after the Change, several families often ate and cooked together. Only the young people at that time thought it couldn't be the old way anymore. For people who were garden workers and who had never cooked, it was a shock. People had to get stoves who had never had one before."

—Mrs. Henry Moershel, Homestead.

Ham Baked in Bread
Jack and Doris Hahn

one recipe basic bread dough   melted butter
14-pound precooked ham   1 egg, beaten

Roll out one-half of the dough to about 15 inches in diameter, or large enough to cover the bottom and 2/3 up the sides of the ham. Place on a large greased baking sheet. With a brush, or your fingers, use water to moisten 2 to 3 inches of the outer edge of the dough circle. Place the ham in the center of the dough. Roll out the second half of the dough to same size and place over the ham. Pull the bottom dough up over the edge of top dough and press hard all around to make the dough stick together. Brush the entire ball with melted butter to keep the dough soft. Let rise in warm place about 45 to 60 minutes or until double. Seal any cracks in the dough using a little water and pressing the cracks together. Brush the entire ball with the beaten egg and bake at 375° to 400° for 1 hour and 45 minutes. Cover lightly with foil if it begins to brown too much before the baking time is up.

Amana girls photographed wearing their bonnets, circa 1915.

Memories of the Community Kitchen
By Emma Setzer
(1897-1987)

Photo by Joan Liffring-Zug

Aunt (Tante) *Emma Setzer with granddaughter
Caroline Setzer, early 1970s.*

There were six kitchens in South Amana and two in Upper South. From thirty to sixty would eat at each kitchen. Sometimes there would be a family with children, and that would make a larger group. And some would have more of the hired men.

My mother was a wonderful kitchen manager. There were three Colby girls and two of us, and on Thanksgiving Day we were the staff of the kitchen. I was seven; my sister was two years older.

We put down the chicken soup to be done for the time when everyone came from the church—everything ready. Oh my, that was quite a responsibility to have that big boiler with chickens cooking away. We'd have to get the rice ready in time and get it cooked so it was nice. We had to bring the chickens out of the broth and pick them off the bones—no bones in there! It had to be done right.

In the kitchen, girls all started to help regularly at about age fourteen. We washed all the tomatoes. There were two or three garden ladies and they'd pick them and bring them up from the gardens way down there. They were all standing around the pump. We washed them, the tomatoes and the cucumbers. We had them by the barrel. At times my mother had thirty barrels in the basement that she'd have to wash off every evening.

Every village dried apples, too. Every kitchen raised onions to be sold in the fall. They'd be shipped to Chicago—from 300 to 800 sacks a kitchen. The first garden lady would come and say, "This week we have to do the onions." We'd find the day when there was not too much to do in the kitchen, and we'd get up early and work an hour before breakfast. The usual everyday schedule was breakfast at six, the noon meal at 11:30, and evenings at 6:30. There was a nine o'clock morning coffee break and a three o'clock afternoon coffee break—just coffee and bread and radishes and cheese or something like that.

We learned to put up everything, dried apples, dried kale—I have some kale out in the garden yet. We'd go down to Middle and dry bushels of kale at the woolen mills in their dryer. We'd bring it back in wooden barrels and store it in the attic and it would be used as greens in the winter—spinach.

We bought the peaches. That was a holiday food, because there were plenty of grapes and apples and ground cherries. We used to make ground cherry pie or kuchen. For a holiday or a wedding we'd have peach kuchen. Whoever's kitchen it was, the bride did the kuchen and she invited the others, like my mother, to help roll out yeast dough for those peach kuchens.

Because there were three girls, one was cook, one was dishwasher, and the third was table-waiter. Each had her work for the week. You knew just what you had to do and you worked accordingly.

Amana house blessing.

Rabbit
Emma Setzer

Mrs. Setzer saved her kitchen scraps for her neighbor's rabbits, so they gave her one. She prepared it when Penfield Press's publisher came to supper. Mrs. Liffring-Zug said, "It was great."

1 medium-sized rabbit	1/2 bay leaf
2 to 3 eggs, well beaten	2 to 3 peppercorns
flour	1/4 onion chopped
1/2 cup water or more	flour or cornstarch
1/2 cup vinegar	salt and pepper to taste

Cut up rabbit into serving pieces and dip in beaten eggs, then in flour. Fry a nice deep brown and put in heavy pan or kettle. Add water and vinegar and simmer gently for several hours. Add bay leaf, peppercorns, and onion to simmering rabbit. When done, thicken gravy with flour or cornstarch. Season to taste and serve.

Beer Sauce for Bratwurst
Carl and Fern Oehl

1 small can tomato paste	1/2 green pepper, diced
1/2 cup catsup	several bits chopped, fresh garlic
1 cup tomato juice	dash of Worcestershire sauce
1 can beer	

This is a family-sized recipe with ingredients mixed together and heated to simmering stage. After individual *Bratwurst* have been thoroughly cooked and nicely browned, place them in the prepared heated sauce until serving time. The preparation may be reused and will keep in your refrigerator in a glass or plastic container. The flavorful sauce is designed for group servings of Amana *Bratwurst* for banquets or for the home chef who specializes in outdoor cookery.

Spareribs with Spaetzle
Colony Inn

2 pounds pork spareribs
2 pounds pork sausage

6 large potatoes, peeled and cut
into large chunks
Spaetzle (See below.)

Cook spareribs in large pot of water for 20 minutes. Add potatoes and sausage and cook until done. Drop *Spaetzle* batter by teaspoonfuls into boiling mixture and cook 7 to 10 minutes.

Spaetzle

3 eggs
1 cup milk

1 teaspoon salt
2 cups flour

Beat eggs and add milk. Gradually add flour and salt, beating well. It should be a thick batter, but not stiff.

German Breslauer Steak
Seven Villages Restaurant, Little Amana, Interstate-80

1 1/2 pounds ground veal
1 1/2 pounds ground pork
1/4 cup minced chives
1/2 cup minced onion

2 teaspoons salt
1/4 teaspoon pepper
1/2 teaspoon nutmeg

Mix together and portion out in patties. Fry in frying pan or on grill until well done. Top with mushroom gravy and serve. Serves four to six.

Photo by Joan Liffring-Zug

South Amana, 1970s.

Liver Dumplings
Florence Rettig Schuerer

Dumplings

1 pound liver, ground	1 cup flour
2 cups bread crumbs	salt and pepper to taste
1 egg	1 onion

Topping

4 tablespoons butter	1/2 cup dry bread crumbs

Mix liver, bread crumbs, egg, flour, salt and pepper, and onion. Drop one teaspoon of mixture at a time into boiling salt water. Boil 15 minutes and remove dumplings to serving dish. Brown bread crumbs in butter and use as topping. Serves four.

Quick Sauerbraten
Helen Kraus

Skips marinating, finished with "snaps."

4 to 5 pound round/rump roast	1 cup red wine vinegar
1/2 cup oil	3 cups water
1/2 cup chopped onion	1/2 cup packed brown sugar
2 teaspoons salt	12 gingersnap cookies,
2 tablespoons mixed pickling spices	crushed

Brown roast in oil in heavy skillet. Pour off oil and add onion, salt, spices, vinegar, water, and sugar. Simmer 3 to 4 hours, until meat is tender. Remove meat and keep it warm. Strain liquid and measure 4 cups of the broth into the skillet. Add gingersnaps. Cook and stir until smooth and slightly thickened. Serves eight.

Desserts

Cream Puffs
Brick Haus Restaurant

Cream Puffs:
1 cup water
1/2 cup butter
1 cup flour
4 eggs

Vanilla Filling:
3/4 cup sugar
3 tablespoons cornstarch
1/4 teaspoon salt
2 cups milk, divided
2 egg yolks
1 tablespoon butter
1 teaspoon vanilla

For Cream Puffs: In a pan, heat water and butter to a rolling boil. Add all the flour at one time and stir vigorously over low heat until mixture leaves the sides of pan and forms a ball (about 1 minute). Remove from heat. Thoroughly beat in eggs one at a time until mixture is smooth. Drop from spoon onto ungreased baking sheets. Bake at 400° about 30 to 40 minutes, until golden brown and puffy. Cool slowly. Split puffs, fill with cream filling and sprinkle with powdered sugar.

For Vanilla Filling: In a pan, combine sugar, cornstarch, and salt. Add 1 1/2 cups milk. Cook until a thick custard. Beat egg yolks and add them to the remaining 1/2 cup of milk. Add egg mixture to custard and cook 2 minutes longer. Add butter and vanilla. Cool and fill puffs.

For a chocolate filling: Follow the above directions but increase sugar to 1 cup. Along with the milk, add 2 1-oz.-squares of unsweetened chocolate.

Florence and Walter Schuerer have baked pies together every Sunday morning for over forty-five years.

Colony Rhubarb

There are many variations of rhubarb pies, a specialty of the Amanas. Florence Schuerer uses only fresh green rhubarb from the garden for her pies, but rhubarb can be frozen for an adequate supply year around. Fresh rhubarb is used also for making *piestengel* (rhubarb wine).

Rhubarb Pie

4 cups chopped rhubarb
1 1/2 cups sugar
3 eggs, slightly beaten*
1/4 cup milk or cream

1/8 teaspoon salt
2 tablespoons flour
1 9-inch unbaked pie shell

Combine rhubarb, sugar, eggs, milk and salt and mix well. Sprinkle flour over bottom of pie shell. Add rhubarb mixture. Bake at 375° about 1 hour. Can top with crumb topping before baking or meringue after baking. Can also cover with a top crust. Variation: 1 cup of sliced strawberries, raspberries, or blueberries can be added to rhubarb.
*Note: Use only egg yolks if meringue topping is desired.

Crumb Topping

3/4 cup flour
1/2 cup oats

1/2 cup packed brown sugar
1/2 cup butter

Combine until crumbly. Sprinkle on top of rhubarb before baking.

No-Fail Cooked Meringue

1 tablespoon sugar
1 tablespoon cornstarch
1/2 cup water

3 or 4 egg whites
1 tablespoon sugar per egg white

Put sugar, cornstarch, and water in saucepan. Cook mixture until thick and clear, stirring constantly. Set aside. Beat eggs until frothy, adding sugar slowly. Continue beating until very stiff. Remove beater and slowly stir in the cooked mixture. Mix it gently. Do not beat in or meringue will be tough. Spread on filling and bake at 350° for 12 to 15 minutes or until lightly browned. Makes enough meringue for one pie.

Chocolate Cookies
From the late Oma Herrmann

8 eggs
4 cups sugar
1 1/2 cups butter

1 1/2 cups cocoa
3 teaspoons baking powder
5 to 6 cups flour

Stir eggs, sugar, and butter for one-half hour if not using mixer. Blend in flour, baking powder and cocoa. Drop by teaspoonfuls on lightly greased cookie sheet. Bake in 325° oven for 8 to 10 minutes.

Oma Moershel's Apple Dumplings

Bill Zuber's Restaurant, Homestead, was founded by Bill and Connie Zuber after Bill's major league baseball career ended in 1949. One of the four dining rooms features pictures and memorabilia of Bill's years as a pitcher for world and national championship teams. This recipe is from Mrs. Henry (Oma) Moershel, mother of Connie Zuber.

3 tablespoons cold butter
4 cups flour, sifted
1 egg, beaten
1 cup sour cream
1 teaspoon salt
1 tablespoon sugar
1 teaspoon flour

1 teaspoon soda
1 tablespoon water
20 apples, peeled and cored
sugar
cinnamon
butter
1/4 cup boiling water

Cut butter into flour. Mix egg, sour cream, salt and sugar together and add 1 teaspoon flour. Dissolve soda in 1 tablespoon water and mix ingredients together. Handling very lightly and as little as possible, roll dough into two sheets as for pie crust. Then cut into 6 or 7-inch squares, making about 20 squares. Put one apple on top of each square. Sprinkle sugar, dash of cinnamon, and a dab of butter over each apple. Fold corners of square over each apple and place in greased baking dish. Sprinkle with more sugar, butter and cinnamon. Put 1/4 cup of boiling water in bottom of dish and bake at 375° until apples are soft and dumpling is golden brown. Serve with sweet cream. Makes twenty dumplings.

Bread Pudding
Florence Rettig Schuerer

Florence says *Bread Pudding* requires a coarse, porous one-pound loaf of bread. This recipe, typical of those used in the community kitchens, serves about 35 people. For family use, you may use one-third of the ingredients and bake it in a 9x9x2-inch pan, or use one-half of the ingredients and bake it in a 9x13x2-inch pan

1 loaf of bread (3 days old)	12 cups cold milk
24 eggs	butter to dot on top
3 cups sugar	

Break bread into bite-sized pieces. Put into oblong pan (12x18x2-inch). Beat eggs and sugar lightly, add cold milk and pour over bread. Dot with butter and bake in a 375° oven till custard is set. Do not heat milk before mixing. We top it with lemon sauce, cherries or strawberries.

Old-Fashioned Jelly Roll
Madeline Schuerer Schulte

3 eggs (1/2 to 2/3 cup)	1 teaspoon baking powder
1 cup granulated sugar	1/4 teaspoon salt
1/3 cup water	about 2/3 cup jelly
1 teaspoon vanilla	powdered sugar
1 cup cake flour	

Heat oven to 375°. Line jelly roll pan with aluminum foil or wax paper; grease. In small bowl, beat eggs about five minutes. Pour eggs into larger mixing bowl; slowly beat in granulated sugar. Turn down speed of mixer to low; blend in water and vanilla. Gradually add flour, baking powder and salt, beating until smooth. Pour into pan, spreading to corners.

Bake approximately 15 minutes. To test, insert toothpick in center until pick comes out clean. Loosen cake from pan, edges first, invert on towel sprinkled with powdered sugar. Remove foil and trim edges if needed. While hot, roll cake and towel from narrow end. Cool on wire rack. Unroll cake; remove towel. Spread jam or jelly over cake. Roll up; sprinkle top and sides with powdered sugar. Yields about ten servings.

Prestele lithograph of the Whitesmith Gooseberry
in the collection of the Museum of Amana History.

Gooseberry Pie

Pastry for a 9-inch 2-crust pie
1 cup sugar
1/3 cup flour

1 tablespoon lemon juice
4 cups gooseberries
2 tablespoons butter

Line a 9-inch pie plate with half the pastry. Mix the sugar, flour, and lemon juice with gooseberries. Turn into the pie plate. Dot with butter and cover with top crust, either plain or lattice top. Bake at 425° for 35 to 45 minutes.

Blackberry Cream Pie
Madeline Schuerer Schulte

1 cup sugar
1 8-oz. carton commercial
   sour cream
3 tablespoons all-purpose flour
1/8 teaspoon salt
4 cups fresh blackberries

1 unbaked 9-inch pastry shell
1 tablespoon sugar
1/4 cup fine dry bread crumbs
1 tablespoon sugar
1 tablespoon butter or
   margarine, melted

Combine first 4 ingredients, stir well. Place blackberries in pastry shell. Sprinkle 1 tablespoon sugar over berries. Spread sour cream mixture over berries. Combine bread crumbs, 1 tablespoon sugar, and butter; sprinkle over top. Bake at 375° for 45 to 50 minutes or until center is firm.

Note: Originally this was a custard served in the community kitchens. In earlier years a double-crust pie was used. Raspberry or currant sauce was served on top.

Ground Cherry Pie

Wild and garden-grown ground cherries were plentiful during the community kitchen era. They are not gathered or cultivated as widely today so are not commonly found in the marketplace, but they are a taste treat when available.

1/2 cup water
1 teaspoon lemon juice
1/4 teaspoon salt

2 cups ground cherries
1 cup sugar
2 tablespoons cornstarch

Prepare an 8-inch pie shell, do not bake. In a saucepan combine water, lemon juice and salt. Bring to a boil and add cherries. In a small bowl, mix sugar and cornstarch together. Gradually add to ground cherries and water mixture, stirring constantly. Simmer until thick; cool slightly. Pour mixture into pie shell and bake at 375° for 30 to 35 minutes.

Apple Pie with Sour Cream
Madeline Schuerer Schulte

If you substitute fresh pears for apples you have Bavarian Pear Pie.

1/3 cup + 2 tablespoons flour
1/3 cup + 3/4 cup sugar
1 1/4 teaspoons cinnamon
1/8 teaspoon salt
1 egg
1/2 teaspoon vanilla

1 cup sour cream
6 medium-sized apples, peeled,
   cored and sliced
1 9-inch pie shell, unbaked
   and chilled
1/4 cup butter

Preheat oven to 400°. In a bowl, sift together 2 tablespoons of the flour, 3/4 cup of the sugar, 3/4 teaspoon cinnamon and the salt. Stir in the egg, vanilla and sour cream. Fold in the apples and spoon mixture into pie shell. Bake 15 minutes, then reduce oven temperature to 350° and bake 30 minutes longer.

    Meanwhile, combine the remaining flour, sugar and cinnamon. With a pastry blender or fingertips, blend in the butter until mixture is crumbly. Increase the oven temperature to 400°. Sprinkle bread crumb mixture over the pie and bake 10 minutes longer.

Red Raspberry Pie
Emaline Bendorf

3 cups raspberries
3 tablespoons quick-cooking tapioca
2 tablespoons flour
1 1/2 cups sugar
pie crust for 9-inch, two-crust pie
1 tablespoon butter

Mix fruit, tapioca, flour, and sugar. Pour into 9-inch pie pan lined with unbaked crust. Dot with butter and adjust top crust. Bake at 450° for 15 minutes.

*Jordan Hans Heusinkveld
by an Amana garden.*

Date Honey Bars
Erma Kellenberger

3 eggs
1 cup honey
1 1/2 cups sifted flour
1/2 teaspoon salt

1 teaspoon baking powder
2 cups ground dates
1 cup ground nutmeats
powdered sugar

Beat eggs well. Gradually beat in honey. Sift flour, salt and baking powder. Stir into egg mixture. Stir in dates and nutmeats. Place in a greased and floured 9x13-inch pan. Bake at 350° for about 30 minutes. When cool, cut cake into bars and roll in powdered sugar. Wrap bars individually in waxed paper. Makes 42 bars.

Honey Cookies from the Community Kitchen
Erna Noé Conrow

2 tablespoons soda
1/4 cup brandy
1 quart honey
1 pound brown sugar

4 eggs, well-beaten
2 cups coarsely ground nuts
1/2 cup candied citron peel
10 cups flour

Dissolve soda in brandy. Heat honey, add sugar. When cooled, add eggs, soda, nuts, citron peel, and flour. Let stand overnight. Place dough on floured board and knead well. Take part of dough, form into rolls about 2 inches in diameter and slice off the cookies 1/4 inch thick. Place on greased cookie sheet and bake in 350° oven for about 10 minutes.

Cutting ice, early 1900s.

Grape Tapioca Pudding with Vanilla Sauce
Florence Rettig Schuerer

Pudding:
1 1/2 cups grape juice
1 cup water

3 tablespoons quick tapioca
1/4 cup sugar

Vanilla Sauce:
1 egg
1/2 cup sugar
2 cups milk

1 teaspoon vanilla
1 tablespoon cornstarch

Pudding: Combine the fruit juice and water, and heat. Add the tapioca and sugar. Boil for 3 minutes. Chill in a 9x5-inch loaf pan. Cut into squares to serve.

Vanilla Sauce: Beat the egg and sugar. Add the milk, vanilla, and cornstarch. Cook for 5 minutes. Chill until cold. Serve on top of the pudding.

Amana-Style Marzipan

2 1/4 cups brown sugar
4 eggs
3 1/2 to 4 cups flour
1 teaspoon soda
1 teaspoon cinnamon

Stir eggs and sugar one-half hour (less if using mixer). Blend in flour, soda and cinnamon. Chill several hours or until firm enough to roll. Roll out on lightly floured board to 1/8-inch thickness and cut with floured cookie cutter. Let stand overnight. Bake on greased baking sheets in 325° oven for 6 to 8 minutes.

Photo by Joan Liffring-Zug

Folk art doll dressed in fabric from the Calico Factory, by Marie Schneider of West Amana.

"The children are kept at school between the ages of six and thirteen. From half-past nine until eleven... they knit gloves, wristlets, or stockings. Boys as well as girls are required to knit. One of the teachers said to me that this work kept them quiet, gave them habits of industry, and kept them off the streets and from rude play."

—*From* The Communistic Societies of the United States, *by Charles Nordhoff, 1875.*

Bertha M. H. Shambaugh photographs

The Amana Cake Traditions

For generations, brides have received a shower of wedding cakes baked by family and friends of the Amana Colonies. When Madeline Schuerer Schulte was married she received over 120 cakes at the reception. It is customary to have the same kinds of cakes brought to a lunch following a funeral. Favorites are White, Chocolate, Marble Cake, Burnt Sugar, Angel Food, and Poppy Seed.

Burnt Sugar Cake

1 1/2 cups sugar, divided
1/2 cup boiling water
2/3 cup butter
1 teaspoon vanilla extract
2 eggs, separated

3 cups sifted cake flour
3 teaspoons baking powder
1 teaspoon salt
1 cup milk
caramel frosting, pecan halves

Heat 1/2 cup sugar slowly in small saucepan, stirring. When sugar is melted and begins to smoke, add water slowly and carefully, stirring. Cook until syrup measures 1/2 cup, stirring until sugar is dissolved. Cool. Cream butter; add 1 cup sugar gradually, beating until light and fluffy. Add vanilla, then yolks, one at a time, beating thoroughly after each. Stir in syrup. Add dry ingredients alternately with milk; beat until smooth. Beat egg whites until stiff and fold into flour mixture. Pour into 3 round 9-inch layer pans, greased and floured, lined on the bottom with wax paper. Bake at 375°, about 20 minutes. Cool and frost. Top with nuts.

Caramel Frosting

2 tablespoons butter
1/3 cup cream
2/3 cup brown sugar, packed

1/8 teaspoon salt
2 drops vanilla
3 cups sifted powdered sugar

Combine first 4 ingredients in saucepan and bring to a boil. Remove from heat and add vanilla. Gradually add powdered sugar and blend until it is of spreading consistency.

Above: Alma's Wash House, Homestead, 1965.
Below: Amana Residence, 1965. The back of the house was originally wood
frame. This building uniquely combines the three main building materials
used in the historic Amanas: brick, sandstone and wood.

Serving Strawberry Shortcake

Sponge cake or a yellow cake can be served as Strawberry Shortcake. At the Brick Haus Restaurant, Florence Schuerer serves, in a one-cup size bowl, a small piece of yellow cake topped with strawberries, a small dip of ice cream and a little whipped cream (or non-dairy cream) for accent.

Poppy Seed Cake

1 1/2 cups sugar
2 sticks butter
4 eggs, separated
1/3 cup poppy seeds

1 teaspoon baking soda
1 cup sour cream
2 cups flour, sifted
powdered sugar

In a mixing bowl, cream the sugar and butter until light in color and fluffy. Beat the egg yolks and add to the mixture with the poppy seeds. In a small bowl, dissolve the baking soda in the sour cream. Add to the sugar and egg yolk mixture alternately with the sifted flour. Beat the egg whites until stiff. Fold into the batter. Bake for 1 hour at 350° in an ungreased 10-inch tube pan or Bundt pan. Cool. Remove from the pan. Frost with favorite frosting. whipped topping, or dust with powdered sugar. Cover tightly and let stand a day so the flavor matures.

Sponge Cake

3 eggs
3/4 cup sugar
1 cup milk
1 3/4 cups flour
1/2 teaspoon salt

3 teaspoons baking powder
4 tablespoons melted butter
3 cups raspberries
1/4 cup sugar

Beat eggs; add 3/4 cup sugar gradually and beat until well blended. Beat in milk. Combine flour, salt, and baking powder; add to egg mixture and beat until smooth. Stir in melted butter. Pour into greased 9x13-inch pan. Sprinkle berries evenly over batter, then sprinkle with sugar. Bake at 375° for 25 minutes. Note: If using frozen berries, thaw partially and drain juice. May need to add to baking time. Pie filling may be used by spooning in rows atop batter. Serves twelve to fifteen.

White Cake

2 3/4 cups sifted flour
4 teaspoons baking powder
3/4 teaspoon salt
4 egg whites
1 1/2 cups sugar, divided

3/4 cup shortening
1 cup + 2 tablespoons milk
1 teaspoon vanilla
1/2 teaspoon almond extract

Sift flour, baking powder, and salt together. Beat egg whites until foamy. Add 1/2 cup of the sugar gradually and continue beating only until meringue will hold up in soft peaks. Cream shortening thoroughly. Add remaining 1 cup sugar and cream together until light and fluffy. Add flour alternately with milk, beating after each addition until smooth. Mix in flavoring then add meringue and beat thoroughly into batter. Pour batter into two 9-inch layer pans, greased and floured, and which have been lined on bottoms with wax paper. Bake at 350° for 30 to 35 minutes. Frost with a butter cream or fluffy frosting.

Daffodil Cake

A lovely silver and gold cake!

1 cup egg whites
1/2 teaspoon salt
1 teaspoon cream of tartar
1 cup sugar

1 cup sifted flour
1 teaspoon vanilla
4 egg yolks
grated rind of 1/2 orange

Beat egg whites with salt until frothy. Add cream of tartar and beat until stiff, but not dry. Gradually add sugar, and beat until very stiff and glossy. Fold in flour in thirds. Add vanilla. Beat egg yolks until thick and lemon-colored. Divide batter, and fold egg yolks and rind into half. Put by tablespoonfuls into an ungreased 9 or 10-inch tube pan, alternating the yellow and white mixtures. Bake at 300°, about 1 hour. Invert on rack to cool. Remove from pan and frost top and sides of cake with a lemon or butter cream frosting.

The Stern *(Star)* Cake *served at wedding celebrations was baked in a star-shaped tin mold. The molds were created by the tinsmith and no two were exactly alike.*
Drawing by Diane Heusinkveld.

Chocolate Layer Cake

4 oz. unsweetened chocolate
1/2 cup butter
1 cup water
2 eggs
1 cup sour cream

2 cups sugar
1 1/2 teaspoons vanilla
2 cups sifted cake flour
1 1/4 teaspoons baking soda
1/2 teaspoon salt

Combine chocolate, butter and water in top of double boiler and heat over simmering water until chocolate is melted. In large bowl beat eggs. Add sour cream, sugar and vanilla. Beat in chocolate mixture. Mix flour, baking soda, and salt and add to batter in 3 additions. Batter will be fairly thin. Pour into greased and floured 8-inch round pans. Bake at 350° for 30 to 40 minutes. Cool in pans about 10 minutes before turning out on racks. When cold, frost with Chocolate Cream Cheese Frosting between layers, on the top and on sides. Sprinkle with chopped nuts if desired.

Chocolate Cream Cheese Frosting

4 oz. unsweetened chocolate, melted
4 oz. cream cheese, softened
1 1/2 teaspoons vanilla

4 1/2 cups sifted powdered sugar
6 to 8 tablespoons milk, orange
  juice or coffee

Beat chocolate, cream cheese and vanilla together. Add sugar. Add liquid slowly, beating until desired spreading consistency.

Plum Cake

3 3/4 cups flour
1 teaspoon baking powder
2 eggs

1 3/4 cups sugar, divided
3/4 cup butter
3 1/2 pounds fresh plums

Sift flour and baking powder onto a large board or clean countertop. Make a hollow in the middle. Crack eggs into hollow, add 3/4 cup sugar and stir. Scatter dots of butter over flour and knead all ingredients together until dough is smooth and soft. Refrigerate for 30 minutes. Wash and pit plums, slitting them in half so that they lie flat, yet are still connected. Roll dough out onto greased jellyroll pan. Cover dough with overlapping rows of plums. Sprinkle with 1/2 cup sugar and bake at 350° for 30 minutes. Remove from oven and sprinkle with remaining sugar. Serve with whipped cream.

Blackberry Cake
Brick Haus Restaurant

3 cups flour
2 cups sugar
1 teaspoon salt
1 teaspoon ground nutmeg
1 teaspoon cinnamon
1 teaspoon ground cloves
2 eggs

1 cup butter, melted
1 cup buttermilk
1 1/2 cups fresh blackberries
1 tablespoon baking soda
1/2 cup chopped walnuts
1/2 cup raisins

Combine flour, sugar, salt, nutmeg, cinnamon, and cloves in a large mixing bowl. Add eggs, butter, buttermilk, and blackberries. Beat for 1 minute at medium speed. Stir in soda, walnuts, and raisins. Spoon batter into a greased and floured 10-inch tube pan. Bake at 350° for 55 to 60 minutes, or until cake tests done.

Fruit Cake
Bill Zuber's Restaurant

1 cup milk
1 1/2 cups sugar, divided
1 tablespoon salt
1 cake compressed yeast
1 cup lukewarm water
6 cups sifted flour, divided
6 tablespoons shortening, melted

3 tablespoons butter, melted
2 cups sliced apples, rhubarb,
    peaches or pitted cherries
2 tablespoons flour
1 egg, beaten
2 tablespoons cream

Scald milk, 1/2 cup sugar, and salt together. Cool until lukewarm. Dissolve yeast in lukewarm water and add to cooled milk. Add 3 cups of flour and beat until smooth. Add melted shortening and remaining flour. Knead well. Place in a greased bowl, cover and let rise until double in bulk, about 3 hours.

This makes enough dough for five 9-inch cakes. Store extra dough in refrigerator. Roll out 1/5 of quantity and place in a greased 9-inch pie plate; make a high rim of dough around outside. Brush with butter and sprinkle with 1/4 cup sugar. Let rise. Press prepared fruit close together into dough. Sprinkle remaining 3/4 cup of sugar and flour over fruit. Before baking combine beaten egg and cream and spoon over fruit. Cover cake with a pan and bake for 10 minutes at 425°, then remove pan from top and continue baking at same temperature for another 25 minutes.

Family gathering walnuts in the Amana woods, early 1900s.

Sour Cream Lemon Pound Cake

1 cup butter
3 cups sugar
6 eggs
1/4 cup lemon juice
1 tablespoon grated lemon rind

3 cups flour
1/2 teaspoon soda
1/2 teaspoon salt
1 cup sour cream

Cream butter and sugar. Add eggs one at a time, beating well after each. Add lemon juice and rind. Mix flour, soda and salt together and add alternately with sour cream to the creamed mixture. Pour into greased and floured 10-inch angel food pan (16 cup size). Bake at 325° for 1 hour and 30 minutes, or until it tests done. Cool 15 minutes before turning out on rack to cool.

Variations:
Orange juice and grated orange rind can be substituted for lemon.

1/4 cup poppy seed or 1/2 cup finely chopped pecans or walnuts can be added.

If desired a lemon glaze can be poured over cake.

Lemon Glaze

2 cups powdered sugar
1/4 cup melted butter

2 tablespoons grated lemon rind
1/4 cup lemon juice

Mix all ingredients together and beat until of spreading consistency.

Colony Bees

In communal times each village had a beekeeper, often the man who was also the schoolteacher. Instead of jam for their snacks, children in the *Kinderschule* were served bread with honey, when available.

Even today there are beekeepers in the Amanas. Honey is used primarily for cookies. Some cooks substitute honey for sugar or liquids. The proportions suggested are: 3/4 cup honey to 1 cup sugar.

Angel Food Cake

1 cup flour
1 cup egg whites
1 teaspoon cream of tartar

1/4 teaspoon salt
1 1/4 cups sugar
1 teaspoon vanilla extract

Sift the flour several times. Beat egg whites until frothy. Add cream of tartar and salt; beat until stiff, but not dry. Gradually beat in sugar. Add vanilla. Fold in the flour in parts. Pour into an ungreased 9-inch tube pan; bake in moderate oven, 325°, about 1 hour. Invert pan on rack. Let stand until cold. Serve plain or spread top with chocolate glaze.

Variation: For a Chocolate Angel Food Cake use the above recipe, but substitute 1/4 cup cocoa for 1/4 cup of the flour. Sift cocoa with the flour. Proceed as above; cool. Spread top of cake with chocolate glaze.

Nut Cake

Nut cakes are among the favorites at Amana wedding receptions.

1 cup soft butter
1 3/4 cups sugar
1 teaspoon vanilla extract
3 eggs and 1 egg yolk
3 cups sifted flour

2 teaspoons baking powder
3/4 teaspoon salt
3/4 cup milk
1 cup finely chopped nuts

Cream butter; gradually add sugar. Beat until light and fluffy. Add vanilla. Add eggs and yolk, one at a time, beating thoroughly after each addition. Add sifted dry ingredients alternately with milk, beating until smooth. Fold in nuts. Pour into greased 9-inch tube pan, lined on bottom with wax paper. Bake in 375° oven for 1 hour, or until done. Cool in pan for 10 minutes, remove to rack.

Photo by Joan Liffring-Zug, 1968

Amana furniture makers passed down their skills from father to son.
The Amana walnut rocker, shown here in the workroom of
the Amana Furniture Shop, is a particular favorite.

Carrot Cake with Cream Cheese Frosting

3 cups flour
2 to 2 1/2 cups sugar
2 teaspoons baking powder
1/2 to 1 teaspoon salt
1 teaspoon baking soda
2 teaspoons cinnamon

1 1/2 cups oil
3 eggs, beaten
1 8-oz. can crushed pineapple
1 teaspoon vanilla
2 cups peeled and grated carrots
1 cup pecans, chopped

Preheat oven to 325°. Sift together flour, sugar, baking powder, salt, baking soda and cinnamon. In a mixing bowl, combine the oil, eggs, pineapple (and pineapple juice). Beat in the dry ingredients. Mix in the vanilla, carrots, and pecans. Pour the batter into a tube pan. Bake at 325° for 1 1/2 hours or until done. Cool and frost with Cream Cheese Frosting.

Cream Cheese Frosting

1 3-oz. package cream cheese
1 teaspoon vanilla

1 1/2 cups powdered sugar

In a mixing bowl, cream all the ingredients together until fluffy. Spread over the top of cooled cake.

Spice Loaf with Raisins

1 cup brown sugar, packed
1 cup raisins
1 1/4 cups water
1/2 cup shortening
1 teaspoon cinnamon
1/2 teaspoon nutmeg

1/2 teaspoon allspice
2 cups flour
1 teaspoon soda
1 teaspoon baking powder
1/2 teaspoon salt

Boil first seven ingredients together for five minutes. Chill. Sift dry ingredients; stir into first mixture. Pour into greased, wax-paper-lined loaf pan, 9x5x3-inches. Bake in 350° oven for one hour. Turn out on rack, remove paper and cool. Serve plain or frost as desired.

Photo by Joan Liffring-Zug

Magdalena (Lena) Schuerer holds a quilt design
at the Museum of Amana History.

Instead of making pieced quilts, the Amana women traditionally used solid fabric on which they drew a pattern across the material. They stitched around the pattern to make the design. In the Communal Era, a bride needed two summer quilts and two winter quilts and twelve sheets. There were no double beds. Six tablecloths, hooked rugs, and doilies were additional household items. Wool for rug weaving came from the Woolen Mill and printed cotton for quilts and clothing came from the Calico Factory. In 1891, the Calico Factory produced 4,500 yards of printed cotton a day for nationwide sales. Lack of dyes from Germany during World War I caused the shutdown of the factory. The Amana Arts Guild, housed in the former High Amana Church building, features craft exhibitions, including quilting, and demonstrations.

Marble Cake

1/2 pound butter
4 eggs, separated
1 3/4 cups sugar
1/2 teaspoon vanilla
4 cups flour

2 teaspoons baking powder
1 cup whole milk
2 squares chocolate
3 tablespoons cream or rum
2 tablespoons sugar

Cream butter and add egg yolks, sugar, and vanilla. Stir for 15 minutes. Sift flour and baking powder and add to batter. Add milk and mix thoroughly. Beat egg whites until stiff and fold into batter. Melt chocolate and blend in cream (or rum) and sugar. Separate 1/3 of the batter into another bowl and add the chocolate. Pour alternating layers of the chocolate and white batter into a greased 10-inch tube pan. Bake at 350° for 1 hour.

Black Walnut Cake

1 cup butter
2 cups sugar
3 cups flour
2 1/2 teaspoons baking powder
1 teaspoon salt

1 teaspoon vanilla
1 cup milk
1 cup chopped black walnuts
4 eggs

Cream the butter and sugar together. Sift flour, baking powder, and salt together and add to creamed mixture. Stir in the vanilla and milk; add the black walnuts. Pour into 3 greased and floured 9-inch-round cake pans. Bake at 375° until cake tests done. Top with white fudge frosting.

White Fudge Frosting with Black Walnuts

3 cups sugar
1 cup milk
1 stick butter

1 teaspoon vanilla
1 cup chopped black walnuts

Combine the sugar and milk in a saucepan and bring to a boil. Cover the saucepan and cook for 5 minutes. Remove from heat and add butter and vanilla. Cool. Beat until thickened and spread on cake. Sprinkle with walnuts between layers and on top of cake.

Many families in the Amana Colonies enjoy this kind of wooden-frame yard swing. This swing gives a view of old village barns in Amana, now the site of the Barn Restaurant. Some swings have grape arbors over them for shade. Traditionally made of oak, this style is made today by Norman Schanz at the Schanz family furniture shop, outside South Amana.

An Old-Fashioned Colony Dinner

"From the days of the community kitchens to the 1980s, a dinner menu of radish salad, boiled beef, spinach and fried potatoes has always been a family favorite at home," says Florence Rettig Schuerer.

Boiled Beef

Boil beef shank or brisket with water and salt until done. Remove and slice for serving, reserving broth for spinach recipe.

Fried Potatoes

Boil potatoes in skins until done. Peel, slice and fry in oil or butter. Sliced onion, salt and pepper may be added.

Spinach

2 cups spinach
2 onions, chopped
1 cup bread crumbs

1/2 stick butter or margarine
1 1/2 cups beef broth

Wash spinach. Blanch until limp. Drain and grind in food chopper. Sauté onions and bread crumbs in butter until onions are done and bread crumbs are brown. Combine with spinach. Add beef broth and mix with spinach until it is of pudding consistency. Cook until the spinach is done.

Radish Salad

2 cups of ground radish
1 scant tablespoon salt
1 tablespoon vinegar

dash of pepper
1/2 cup cream

Mix and let stand one hour before serving.

Photo by Joan Liffring-Zug

*Nostalgic scene of a bygone era. These wheels were photographed in 1969
outside a building that once housed a blacksmith shop in Homestead.*

Above: Brick chicken coop, South Amana.
Below: Old pump house, Homestead.

Visiting the Amanas

Every year the people of the Amana Colonies, Iowa's leading visitor attraction and a national historic landmark, welcome visitors from all over the world. The famous restaurants serving family-style foods featuring German-American specialties, the wineries, woolen mill outlet stores, general stores, gift shops, and other unique shops are open year-around. Historic museums are open spring through fall. All villages except East Amana have visitor-related businesses. East is noted for its picturesque charm.

Little Amana on Interstate-80 at Exit 225, founded by the Amana Society, has a Welcome Center, motel and restaurant, general store, a winery, and woolen mill outlet. Across the street are additional motels and restaurants. All the restaurants, including those in the Colonies, serve traditional family-style German-American meals in addition to short orders. The Colony land and villages begin approximately six miles north of the Interstate. There are bed and breakfast facilities in the villages, particularly in Amana, Homestead and Middle.

Another Welcome Center with exhibition grounds is near the intersection of Highways 151 and 220 in Amana. This is the site of the World Ag Expo, Farm Progress Shows and other large events including balloon rallies. Various Amana villages host art workshops, seasonal festivals and collectors' events. For more information about events, which vary annually, write: Amana Colonies Convention and Visitors Bureau, P.O. Box 303, Amana, Iowa 52203. Phone: (319) 622-7622 or 1-800-245-5465.

The season begins with a *Maifest* in early May. The Middle village park is the site of a Bluegrass Festival, the Amana Festival of the Arts, and the *Oktoberfest*. A woodcrafters' festival, the *Holzfest*, is held at the Colony Village Restaurant, I-80 at Exit 225. An *Eisenfest*, a fair featuring all metals from aluminum to zinc, is held in Amana.

The Amana Arts Guild Center in the High church building offers a traditional Amana communal meal by advance reservation. The Guild features exhibitions of arts and crafts.

The Prelude to Christmas is Main Amana's holiday celebration with candle-lit streets, entertainment, heart-warming hospitality, and special events at the Museum of Amana History.

More Books About Amana and German Americans

German Recipes (this book) $8.95

Amana Colony Recipes: A Collection of Traditional Amana Recipes. $9.95

Guten Appetit from Amana Kitchens: The Amana Preservation Foundation Cookbook
6 x 9 inches, 185 pages, spiral bound, hardcover. $15.50

Seasons of Plenty: Recipes from the Days of the Communal Kitchens
10 1/2 x 8 1/4 inches, 238 pages.$21.95
A project of the Amana Arts Guild, this book of cultural and culinary heritage by Emily Hoppe, illustrated by Rachel Ehrman, tempts the eye as well as the palate. Hardcover.

The Amana Colonies: Seven Historic Villages
8 1/2 x 11 inches, 48 pages. $6.95
Full-color booklet edited by Allyn Neubauer, Amana Society. Produced by Joan Liffring-Zug and John Zug, Penfield Press. Brief history and detailed photo tour of the Amanas today.

The Story of an Amana Winemaker
6 x 9 inches, 48 pages. $9.95
By George Kraus as told to E. Mae Fritz. Instructions on how to make various wines—including Dandelion, Rhubarb, and Tomato. Includes cooking with wine.

A Change and a Parting: My Story of Amana $10.95
5 1/2 x 8 1/2 inches, 364 pages.
By Barbara S. Yambura with Eunice Willis Bodine. Relates the vivid memories of girlhood days in the Amana Colonies before and after the "Great Change."

Amana: The Community of True Inspiration
6 x 9 inches, 416 pages. $9.95
By Bertha M. H. Shambaugh.
This rare book tells about life in the Amanas at the turn of the century. Includes photographs by the author. It is the only book of its kind, written during the Communal Era. Reprint.

Willow Basketry of the Amana Colonies
6 x 9 inches, 96 pages. $8.95
By Joanna E. Schanz. Detailed instructions and illustrations on how to make baskets. Photographs show baskets of the early 1900s as well as today's basketmakers.

The Communistic Societies of the United States: from the Personal Observations of Charles Nordhoff
5 1/2 x 8 1/2, 439 pages. $9.95
An account of the Amanas in 1875 is presented, as well as information on other communal societies.

German-American Life Recipes and Traditions
6 x 9 inches, 208 pages. $12.95
Edited by John D. Zug and Karin Gottier. History of the settlements and traditions of German Americans. Sixteen pages of full-color photographs cover Germans in America. Cover photo shows Amana children. Includes essays about the Amanas, some traditional Amana recipes, and instructions for coloring "Amana-style" Easter eggs.

By mail:
Add $4 shipping for orders up to $25, $5.75 for orders over $25.
(Prices subject to change.)

Penfield Press
215 Brown Street
Iowa City, IA 52245

The Amanas Yesterday:
A Religious Communal Society
Historic Photographs from 1900–1932
Collected by Joan Liffring-Zug.
8 1/2 x 11 inches, 48 pages. $8.95

At one time personal photographs were severely condemned and absolutely forbidden in the Amana Colonies. As the rules of conduct relaxed, many people (particularly men) obtained cameras and began to photograph life in the colonies.

Right: Entertaining visitors. Below: Dr. Christian Herrmann photographed his mother returning from the communal kitchen, 1915. Baskets of food were prepared to take home for the ill, the elderly, and those with small children.

Recipe Index

Photo by Joan Liffring-Zug

Rhubarb crusher, left, and cherry press,
Community Kitchen Museum, Middle Amana.

Below: Time-exposed self portrait and photograph by Dr. Christian Herrmann (at right), when he was a young man, shows the cleaning group at the pharmacy in the mid-1900s. When the elders gradually relaxed the bans against photography, Dr. Herrmann was among a number of men who purchased cameras. He was one of the most gifted of the photographers. His daughter, Ruth Schmieder, carries on his visual talent today in her miniatures and oil paintings. Before the end of the Communal Era, some Amana families had their portraits taken in nearby Marengo.

Photo by Joan Liffring-Zug

*The hands of Mrs. William Foerstner
with lock and key at the historic General Store in High Amana.*

"Behold the work of the old…
Let your heritage not be lost,
but bequeath it as a memory,
treasure and blessing.
Gather the lost and the hidden
and preserve it for thy children."
—Christian Metz